FOR SUCH A TIME AS THIS
WALKING THROUGH CRISIS

SUE CORL

AND CONTRIBUTING AUTHORS

KAELAH BYROM, TYLA KOZUB, NANCY MARTIN

JULIE BRANSTETTER

Crown of Beauty International

For Such a Time as This

All rights reserved.
Copyright © Crown of Beauty International 2020
ISBN-13: 9798694564090
Editor: Kaelah Byrom
Cover Design and Illustration by: Daniel Folta
Library of Congress Control Number: 2018675309
Printed in the United States of America
https://crownofbeautyintl.wixsite.com/crownofbeauty
All Scripture quotation are from the Holy Bible, New International Version® (NIV)

Crown of Beauty International

TABLE OF CONTENTS

Preface..5
Epigraph...7
Part I— The Struggle..8
- *A Confusing Time...9*
- *A New Normal Part I...................................12*
- *A New Normal Part II..................................15*
- *From Ashes to Beauty..................................18*
- *In the Midst of Fear and Uncertainty...........21*
- *What Color Is Your Mood Ring?.................23*
- *Sleepless Nights..26*
- *The Challenge of Changes...........................29*
- *You Are Not Alone......................................32*

Part II — How We Respond...35
- *How Should We Respond to Bad Reports?..........36*
- *Though I Walk Through the Valley....................39*
- *An Encounter with Jesus..................................42*
- *Run to the Father..45*
- *Am I Lavish with Jesus? 48*
- *Solid Rock or Bedrock?...................................51*
- *An Attitude of Expectancy...............................54*
- *The Rewarder of Those Who Seek Him...............57*
- *What Is It?..60*
- *Running Aimlessly or Running Well..................63*
- *Freed from Perfectionism into Grace..................66*
- *Ask for God-given Dreams...............................69*

Part III — How God Responds....................................72
- *Don't You Care?..73*
- *Reveling in His Creation..................................76*

For Such a Time as This

- *Healing from a Tragedy..........................79*
- *God Is My Keeper.................................82*
- *Removal and Replanting.......................84*
- *God's Response to Our Fears.................87*
- *A Beautiful Spring Tree of Hope............89*
- *Shakan! An Unusual Battle Word..........91*
- *He Calls Us to Be Children...................94*

<u>Part IV — Grieving Brings Hope</u>..................................97

- *Not Why, But How?...........................98*
- *God Never Lets Us Go......................100*
- *Hope Beyond the Lament...................103*
- *It's Okay to Not Be Okay...................106*
- *The Beauty of Waiting......................108*
- *The Secret of Contentment.................111*
- *What Is the Meaning of Life?...............114*

Authors..118

Endorsements...120

PREFACE

On March 11th, 2020, the World Health Organization declared COVID-19 a global pandemic. There is no one on this earth who has been untouched by the effects of this virus, as it has influenced every area of our lives; social, economic, and health. And though we had all hoped that it would not last for longer than a few months, it appears that COVID-19 is not going anywhere any time soon. If that statement is not true, it is certainly true that our world has been forever changed.

We, Crown of Beauty International began writing blogs because we were unable to hold conferences and meet formally. We wanted to offer encouragement for our readers during these difficult times as we were all facing COVID-19, but also our own unique struggles. As we continued to write, God made it clear to us that we should be writing a book for times of crisis, trials, and grief. You will get different perspectives from five authors, each of us who has been profoundly touched by and changed as a result of the Lord using trials to bring us closer to our Lord and transformed by His powerful love. We have each included our personal testimonies, interspersed throughout the book so you can see our journey of healing. As you will see, God has used His Word to lift us out of the miry clay and into green pastures.

The title, *For Such A Time as This*, is a phrase that comes straight out of the book of Esther, and its meaning points to God being able to use us in difficult times and bring about His good plans. Though the phrase rings especially true for this season of COVID-19, it applies to all trials. With every season of trouble that we face, God yearns to bring us comfort and hope, and to use us to bring about His perfect plan.

For Such a Time as This

So whether you are reading this shortly after it is published as the pandemic continues to affect our daily lives or five years from now when the next painful challenge appears — We pray that these reflections bring you comfort. We hope that you will hear God speak to you clearly. We pray that this book will be a safe place as you experience pain and grief. We also hope that *For Such a Time as This* will point you to the One who loves you most, and the true hope we have in Jesus.

Crown of Beauty International

A TIME FOR EVERYTHING

Ecclesiastes 3:1-13

There is a time for everything
and a season for every activity under the heavens:
a time to be born and a time to die,
a time to plant and a time to uproot,
a time to kill and a time to heal,
a time to tear down and a time to build,
a time to weep and a time to laugh,
a time to mourn and a time to dance,
a time to scatter stones and a time to gather them,
a time to embrace and a time to refrain from embracing,
a time to search and a time to give up,
a time to keep and a time to throw away,
a time to tear and a time to mend,
a time to be silent and a time to speak,
a time to love and a time to hate,
a time for war and a time for peace.

For Such a Time as This

THE STRUGGLE

Part I

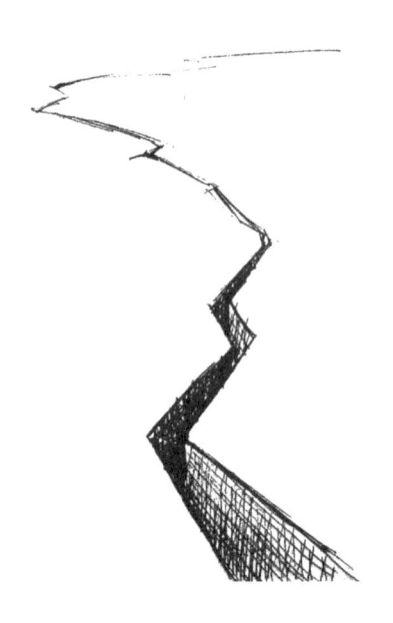

A CONFUSING TIME

Lately, I don't know how to feel. One minute I am full of compassion and want to help those who are suffering. The next minute I find myself in self-protective or self-gratification mode. Should I go to the store and buy food for those in need or should I stay home and protect myself from this dreaded pandemic? Should I send money to help those who have no food, or should I save my $1200 government stimulus check in case this crisis drags on for months? Should I spend money on extra things that bring me comfort, or should I give it away to an organization to feed the hungry children? This pandemic is not the first we have asked ourselves questions torn between compassion and self-preservation, and it won't be the last time. In the season that you're in, do you struggle with these kinds of decisions?

This morning I told God that I didn't even know how to pray. As He is sovereign over the affairs of all, should I pray that He supernaturally stops this pandemic NOW? Or do I pray that He will use this to turn the hearts of people around the world to live in more caring, loving, and God-fearing ways? How do I pray for nations where the leaders govern in corrupt evil ways? In any difficult season, there are many issues, personal and distant, that it can feel impossible to know how to pray.

So what do we do? How do we pray? How do we deal with our conflicting emotions in confusing times? To be honest, there is not an easy answer to this. However, the Scriptures are full of accounts of people wrestling with these same kinds of emotions and decisions. Think about the crisis that Queen Esther went through. She discovered that the chief advisor had convinced the King to annihilate all the Jews. When Esther's cousin, Mordecai, challenged her to beg the king for mercy on behalf of all the Jewish people, she went into self-protective mode. She told Mordecai that she would surely be executed since she could only appear before the king if she was invited to do so. Her cousin confronted her fear with a bold truth:

> "Do not think that because you are in the kings' house you alone of all the Jews will escape. For if you remain silent at this time, relief and deliverance for the Jews will arise from another place, but you and your father's family will perish. And who knows but that you have come to royal position for such a time as this?" (Esther 4:12-14).

So the first principle we see regarding how to deal with confusing times of crisis is to seek out wise mentors. Ask those who have a history of making wise godly decisions. Once Esther made the smart move to listen to her cousin's counsel, her next wise decision was to call the Jewish people to fast and pray for three days before she spoke to the king. It is interesting that when Esther decided to step out in faith in obedience to God's will, her heart changed from fear to sacrificial courage. She boldly said: "And if I perish, I perish" (Esther 4:16). Thus we see the second principle in how to deal with confusing times: pray and ask others to pray for you about how to respond (think and act).

The third principle came up as Esther courageously stepped out in faith to help those in need. She did not act impulsively. In fact, she patiently and carefully acted on behalf of the people. We do not know exactly why she did not tell the king immediately. She wined and dined him twice. He offered her anything she wanted during the first banquet she gave him, but she held back her request. She asked to give him another banquet. Before the second banquet, God orchestrated the king to not be able to sleep and then request to read the chronicles of his reign. Through this, he was reminded of a time when Esther's cousin Mordecai saved the king from an assassination attempt. During the second banquet, Esther revealed the king's advisor, Haman's evil plot to have Mordecai, Esther, and all the Jews killed. With great passion, he had Haman hanged, Mordecai honored, and the Jews protected from being killed.

Thus we see the third principle: step away from your own self-protective or self-gratifying responses and ask God how you can be a servant to others. God may give you ideas of how to encourage and help others during this season. You can trust that He will provide for you as you step out in faith to do His will. Esther is a wonderful example of how to deal with confusing times in a way that is wise, prayerful, self-sacrificing, and God-honoring. May God lead you with His wisdom out of the darkness of confusion and into the light of His assurance.

Today's Bible Reading: Esther
By Sue Corl

For Such a Time as This

A NEW NORMAL

Part I

The phrase *a new normal* has been flying around on social media. As I am writing this, we are in the midst of the Covid-19 pandemic. We are all trying to find a new way to spend each hour of our day while remaining in our homes. In some ways, the Covid-19 government restrictions are providing many of us with a slowed-down pace. This pandemic is just one example of a time when we must adjust to a new normal. Losses of relationships, financial status, job or role changes, or other losses put us in the position of seeking a new normal. Are you in *a new normal* season of life? What has that been like for you? Restful? Lonely? Confusing? Creative? Chaotic? Challenging your sense of worth? Boring or busy?

There is a character in the Bible who experienced a battle which elicited most of these emotions. Remember Jonah's crazy story? Thrown off a ship, only to be swallowed up by a large fish (probably a whale) for three days. Can you even imagine it? Dark. All alone. Little hope of survival. Surrounded by horrible conditions; he faced separation from anyone who knew and cared about him as endless hours passed by and he fought to survive. I cannot even fathom what I would do in that same situation. As I think about those currently suffering in the hospital with Coronavirus, they are probably experiencing many of these same feelings. Read Jonah 2:1-6 if you want to understand some of the pain he was going through.

In the second chapter of Jonah, a beautiful thing happened in Jonah's heart amid his wretched situation. He prayed! But look how he prayed. In Jonah 2:7-9, we see an attitude shift in Jonah;

> "When my life was ebbing away, I remembered you Lord, and my prayers rose to you, to your holy temple. Those who cling to worthless idols forfeit the grace that could be theirs. But I, with a song of thanksgiving, will sacrifice to you. What I have vowed I will make good. Salvation comes from the Lord."

Can you imagine fighting off being strangled by seaweed, struggling to stay away from the stomach acid, and then giving thanks to God! Perhaps in those prayers, he personally met God in a way that completely humbled him and filled him with unexplainable peace. When we have a supernatural encounter in the presence of God, all pain and fear flee. We begin to recognize what really matters; a worshipful, obedient relationship to the one true God. Jonah recommitted himself to the vows he had previously made to God. When we go through catastrophic events, we can either become bitter or hopeless, or we can have a positive paradigm shift in our emotions. Jonah became repentant. He knew he had been disobedient and was running away from God's will. In the belly of a whale, he spent time thinking and praying about the ways he had displeased the Lord, and through that, was reminded of the earlier times when he was more passionate to follow God.

Sisters and brothers, use this time to pour out your hearts to God. Then let the Holy Spirit guide you to reflect on your life. What can you be thankful for? What commitments have you previously made to the Lord that you have not followed through on? Repent of anything that is displeasing to the Lord. Let your *new normal* include a deeper commitment to the Lord of your salvation. Who knows then what God will do? Marvelous things happen when we surrender to the will of God!

Today's Bible Reading: Jonah 1-2
By Sue Corl

A NEW NORMAL

Part II

Hatred . . . Who me? Hatred is a horrible feeling. It is not something that most of us want to feel or admit to. And yet, when we refuse to forgive someone or ourselves, it often comes from a root of hatred. Unknowingly, hatred can be passed down from one generation to another. When we grow up around people who express their hostility toward us, another individual, a group, or even a race, we sadly can take hold of these oppressive perspectives.

None of us are exempt from the temptation to fall into hatred. When injustice falls on our doorstep, the enemy seizes this opportunity to introduce us to this dangerous evil companion. When we are falsely accused, when someone we love is wrongly hurt, when we lose someone we care about; hatred crouches at our door.

Look at the heart of Jonah. A prophet. A servant of God. Yet, a part of his heart was blackened by the cancer of racism.

For Such a Time as This

Growing up in northern Israel in the 8th century B.C., he had listened to the stories of the past brutality of the Ninevites toward the Jews. The prophet Nahum lets us know that these rulers of Assyria were terribly cruel (see Nahum 3:1-4). Monuments from the Assyrians have been excavated in modern-day Iraq that show they would cut off body parts; they even ripped off peoples' skin and displayed it on the city walls. They destroyed nations through acts of violence, deception, and idolatry; their religion was that of Satanic worship. For these reasons, God sent Jonah on a mission to tell them of His intent to judge and destroy them.

Jonah was eager for God's judgment to come upon them. However, he had a hunch that if he went to Nineveh and prophesied, the people would repent, and God would have mercy on them. The seed of racism was deep in his heart. Jonah said he would rather die than see the Ninevites forgiven (see Jonah 4:3). As the story comes to an end, we see the Ninevites repent and Jonah turn his anger and disappointment toward God. The Lord patiently counsels Jonah as to the value of the lives of these 120,000 people.

Though God judges the wicked, he also forgives when they sincerely repent. The Lord held back his judgment on the repentant Ninevites for one hundred twenty years. After that time, they turned back to their wicked ways, and God's wrath fell upon them.

As difficult as it may be, God calls us to forgive our enemies. As I write this, the day is Good Friday when we celebrate and give thanks to God for the greatest gift of love ever given to the world. Completely innocent, Jesus sacrificed his life on the cross, taking the punishment for our sins upon Himself. He did this to open the doors for us to be forgiven and receive an eternal relationship with the living God!

Instead of hatred for His offenders, Jesus said: "Forgive them for they know not what they do" (Luke 23:34). Years before this amazing act of love, God spoke through the prophet Isaiah to let us know of His redemptive provision. "But He was pierced for our transgressions, He was crushed for our iniquities; the punishment that brought us peace was upon Him, and by His wounds, we are healed" (Isaiah 53:5).

Sisters and brothers, turn to God with any feelings of hatred, racism, or unforgiveness. Release these feelings to God. Ask for forgiveness for your bitterness and judgment. Trust the Lord, our Righteous Judge that in His timing, He will deal with the sins of our offenders. Forgive your enemies. "But I (*Jesus*) tell you: love your enemies and pray for those who persecute you that you may be sons and daughters of your Father in heaven" (Matthew 5:44-45). Let us come out of this difficult season with a new normal, a heart of forgiveness and love, even for our enemies.

Today's Bible Reading: Isaiah 53:4-6; Matthew 5:43-48; Jonah 3-4.
By Sue Corl

For Such a Time as This

FROM ASHES TO BEAUTY
the Testimony of Sue Corl

One night as I was putting my ten year old daughter to bed, she asked me, "Mommy, can you tell me a story about something fun that happened to you in school when you were my age." I sat there in silence trying to rack my brain for something that brought laughter to my heart and hers. I could not think of one happy moment from my elementary school experience. I could write volumes of fun times with friends in my neighborhood and with my family, but not school. It sits as one big black hole in my history. I can only guess that this is because school was a continuous painful place for me. This was where I became a target for the cruel teasing of boys who seemed to have a need to build up their self-esteem by tearing down mine. Their barrage of demeaning names left me defenseless to fight off the wounds that tore at my soul. Names like "circus freak, ugly, and pug face" began to define me. Sadly, these lies became what I thought were true about me.

I had everything but a typical childhood. While in my mother's womb, the doctors were fearful that I would be born with no arms or legs. My mother was a pediatric nurse and worked at a hospital where they specialized in caring for cleft palate babies. Therefore, two years later, when I was born with a severe cleft palate, she did not panic, but rather knew without any doubt that God had prepared her for this special child. I was God's chosen baby for her, and she was sure in her heart that God had a special purpose for me on this earth. God had prepared my mother through her nursing training and experience with cleft palate babies to be the perfect caretaker for me.

Crown of Beauty International

I was born with no nose, no palate, and no upper lip. This was 1959 and the medical profession was only just starting to develop procedures to help these children. Before that, children with severe cleft palates would either die or be hidden away from society since they would never be able to speak or eat properly. The doctors had no idea how to close such a huge gap so that I could begin to suck and get nutrition. Despairingly they told my mother there was nothing they could do. I started to lose weight fast and my mother realized that very quickly I would die in that state. At midnight, she checked me out of the hospital so I could go home.

At home, she managed to make a contraption to put on my face and cover the gap and allow me to begin successfully sucking up milk from a bottle. Within three months, my body became stronger, so my mother called the doctor and demanded that he operate and find a way to close the hole. By God's grace, he was successful, and he became the leading doctor of new methodologies to help cleft palate babies, with me as his research project. I was his masterpiece, his showcase.

Years later I learned that in reality, I am God's masterpiece — not because I have a repaired cleft palate, but because I was wonderfully designed in my mother's womb and am being daily molded into the likeness of Christ. Though I had to endure twenty-seven surgeries over the first fifteen years of my life, I see now how this journey has been one of turning years of "ashes" into a story of redemption and beauty.

He has truly done a miraculous work in my heart. My whole way of looking at myself has changed. No longer do I see myself as an ugly, rejectable, or unlovable person. Now I can confidently say that I have been fearfully and wonderfully made. Psalm 139:13-14 and Isaiah 61:3 have become my life verses. I have been endowed with a high calling to glorify our Lord. I have the amazing right to call myself a daughter of the

For Such a Time as This

King of kings. The Word of God has been powerful to renew my mind and bring transformation to my soul. As the lies of the enemy are replaced with the amazing truths of who I am in Christ, the painful memories of my past have been healed and my soul has been restored to become a worshipper, and lover of Jesus, the Satisfier of my soul.

Though not quickly or easily, this transformation has been a journey of healing over the years. My Savior went to the depths of my pain and revealed the lies, sin, and shame that permeated my soul. My Redeemer took the darkness and brought His light of forgiveness, acceptance, deliverance, and love. Out of the ashes has risen beauty.

IN THE MIDST OF FEAR AND UNCERTAINTY

Who is God in the midst of fear and uncertainty? We are all familiar with fear, perhaps increasingly so as we witness panic infiltrate our news, the thoughts, hearts, and behaviors of those around us, and possibly our own as well. It takes only a few moments of glancing at world reports before sadness, uncertainty, and waves of other emotions sweep over us. We have all become increasingly aware of the battle to walk in peace day by day. So who is God in the midst of our fear and uncertainty, and how does He respond to us?

> "Jesus Christ is the same yesterday and today and forever" (Hebrews 13:8).

I've seen this verse posted on several social media platforms this week and I don't think it is a coincidence that many of us are paying attention to this message. Could it be that our God is the same God today as He was before the

For Such a Time as This

crises we face? The same God He was on the days that brought us the most joy? The same God who was trustworthy and true when life was "normal"? The same God who He has always been throughout all of history, both during times of peace and times of great tragedy, turmoil, and death? Could it be that though so much has changed, and the uncertainty is great, God has not changed at all? The truth is, He is still sovereign, still in control, still full of loving-kindness, and compassion!

Look back at Hebrews 13:8. The Prince of Peace is still who He has always been and His invitation is to come and receive each day true peace that is only found in Him. Do not let the circumstances of the world and your life rob you of your peace. God has not changed; He is seated on His throne. He is ready to engage with you and your honest, raw emotions. He is offering you peace in Him. Press in, receive it, and don't let go. Then, share it with those around you and witness the goodness of the Lord!

Today's Bible Reading: Psalm 27; Psalm 46:10
By Nancy Martin

WHAT COLOR IS YOUR MOOD RING?

We all have a longing to be heard and understood. We also long for someone who will empathize and show compassion. Most of us experience up-and-down emotions at some point in our lives. Like many of you who are also facing trials, I find myself at this point. I woke up feeling down and discouraged today. In fact, as I took a walk with Jesus this morning, I imagined myself wearing a mood ring. Have you ever seen one of those? You put it on your finger, and it turns a certain color according to your mood. If I had been wearing a ring this morning, it would have been black! Unsettled, discouraged, weary of it all. But as I continued to pour my heart out to my compassionate Lord, the ring gradually changed colors: gray, amber, green, blue-green, and finally blue. I never quite made it to the ultimate happy color, violet. But blue symbolizes calmness and a feeling of being loved.

How did I get there? I opened-up my emotions to Jesus. I told Him all my frustrations, discouragement, and mixed feelings. I kept talking! (The Lord truly is a good listener.)

For Such a Time as This

Finally, when I got it all out, I stopped to listen. This is the part that many of us miss. We go to the counselor, dump our woes, and then run out of the office without waiting to see and hear the counselor's response. Do you give time for God to respond after you pray, or do you rush off to begin the tasks of your day?

Let us look at a beautiful counseling session in the Scriptures (there are many!). In John 11:1-44, we see the story of Lazarus' death and resurrection. Of course, this is a significant event because the disciples and many others witnessed the power of God to raise one from the dead. This is a precursor to the resurrection of Christ. But there is another meaningful message in this story: Jesus' responses to Martha and Mary. He had a different response for each of them. Jesus knows us to the very core, so He uniquely answers our cries according to the true needs of our hearts. To Martha, He immediately let her know that her brother would be resurrected. He went on to reveal to her that He is the resurrection and the life and that believing in Him will bring eternal life. To Mary, He had a different response; "When Jesus saw her weeping, and the Jews who had come along with her also weeping, He was deeply moved in spirit and troubled. . . Jesus wept" (John 11:33, 35). Many around Jesus were inspired by the love He demonstrated to Mary.

The Lord is an amazing counselor. He wants you to pour out your emotions and thoughts to Him. He can handle whatever emotions you have. Anger, confusion, discouragement. He even is willing to listen to our doubts about Him. Jesus responded to Martha and Mary's doubts with compassion and love. He knew what they needed. Reassurance and truth for Martha. Tears for Mary.

Yes, at times when I go through loss or am counseling one who is grieving, I can sense in my spirit that the Lord is weeping. We can think it is unspiritual to moan at God. Hey

— He already knows how you feel, so be honest with Him. It will be healing for your soul. But do not just "dump and run!" Sit and be still. Allow the Lord to speak to you. You may even feel deep comfort as His Spirit fills you with His love and compassion. Some have said they felt a hug from God or sensed His tears of compassion.

End your time by stating by faith what the Scripture says about the character of God. Here is a good way to end your time with God each time you pray: "Lord, no matter how I feel, I know Your Word tells me that You are good, loving, faithful, and sovereign over all. So I trust You and surrender myself to Your will." This simple prayer will prevent the enemy from getting a stronghold in your heart. And it will bring the honor and glory our Almighty God deserves.

Today's Bible reading: John 11:1-44
By Sue Corl

For Such a Time as This

SLEEPLESS NIGHTS

Have you ever had sleepless nights or been plagued by bad dreams? Has your sleep ever been disrupted by what was going on in the world around you? According to Romans 8:15, we can cry out to our "Abba Father!" Abba is the Aramaic word for father, used by Jesus and Paul to address God with personal intimacy. Abba is our Daddy, a Dad who loves us and has the best for us.

> "So you have not received a spirit that makes you fearful slaves. Instead, you received God's Spirit when He adopted you as His own children. Now we call Him, "Abba, Father" (Romans 8:15, NLT).

His Spirit joins with our spirit to affirm that we are God's children. "And since we are His children, we are His heirs. In fact, together with Christ, we are heirs of God's glory. But if we are to share His glory, we must also share His suffering" (Romans 8:17, NLT).

Crown of Beauty International

Our world is in a time of suffering. So we are affected! How do we deal with the tossing and turning of our souls? The simple answer is to turn your eyes on Jesus. But in difficult times, it is not that easy. Life seems complicated and we are distracted. The enemy is gripping us with fear.

I know for me, this season has been a time of being hit with spiritual warfare at night. For a few weeks, I was upset that I was losing sleep and that God was not delivering me from my sleepless nights. I was being attacked by my thoughts constantly. I was having bad dreams that were making me feel anxious in ways I have never felt before. But as I got people to pray for me, went on long prayer walks, and sought the Lord in His Word, I finally realized He wanted more of my attention. Daddy, the King of the universe wanted to spend more time with me in this unprecedented time.

Every time I sought Him, it was a sweet time, but afterwards, my thoughts would again wander and I would feel anxious. I finally understood the Lord was having me share in His suffering. This is a strange thought, but God has suffered for us in a thousand ways! He understands our pain, anxiety, loneliness, depression, and grief. So in this season, instead of fighting my sleepless nights, I am embracing them. I now ask the Lord to help me to pray for others who are suffering, or others who just need prayer in general. I have been praying for wisdom for our government like never before. I am now asking the Lord to get me up with a song or to make me uncomfortable in my sleep so I will get up and pray as He wants me too.

Jesus had many sleepless nights praying with the Father, His Daddy. God not only wanted to help Jesus know what to do for the following day, but He also wanted alone time with His Son. So if you have trouble sleeping, embrace it! Go to your Daddy who has called you His Daughter and Heir. He so adores you and wants to be with you today and in the

For Such a Time as This

middle of the night!

May the Lord give you a song and hope today. May you rest only in Him. Lord please sustains us with sleep or no sleep! Thank You that You are perfect in all Your ways and always help us through every season, no matter what! I love you, Daddy!

Today's Bible Reading: Romans 8:15-17
By Tyla Kozub

THE CHALLENGE OF CHANGES

Every day we are facing changes at a magnitude we probably have never faced before. Change can be hard. My husband has been known to say, "I like change about as much as a root canal." In reality, no one enjoys going through big changes. They can be unsettling to the mind and the body, and our emotions only follow. In times of transition, waiting, or uncertainty, we secretly wonder, "What can I count on? What will stay the same?" Thankfully, the Scriptures are full of positive examples of how God successfully led His people through massive change.

Our Scripture today is an account of a significant transition Israel went through when Moses was nearing death and Joshua was being groomed to take over. The "wilderness" era was completed. The Promised Land and its huge benefits loomed before them, but the people had to take it by faith; they needed to fight to attain what God had promised them. The good news is God did not leave His people helpless to fend for themselves. Yes, He required their obedience and participation in conquering their enemies, but He also promised that He himself would go before them to drive out their enemies and secure the beautiful land for them!

What were the Israelites feeling at that time? Certainly, they had been loyal to Moses and knew his track-record as one who lived close to God, and who helped them conquer many challenges by obeying the voice of the Lord. Would Joshua be as trustworthy as Moses had been? Joshua was an experienced warrior who had won a major battle for Israel (See Exodus 17:10-13). And it was Joshua who remained in the Lord's presence even long after Moses had left and gone about other business as the community leader (See Exodus 33:11). It was not hard to see that Joshua was the leader God had prepared for them. Still, their opponents seemed so large to them (See Numbers 13:33)!

God knew His people would soon face bigger challenges than they had known in the wilderness. The wilderness had been a season of building their spiritual muscles. Now they had to cross the Jordan to face an unknown enemy. Though times felt uncertain, God would surely not leave His people alone!

Oscar C. Eliason's Got Any Rivers says it this way:

> "Got any rivers you think are uncrossable? Got any mountains you can't tunnel through? God specializes in things thought impossible. And He can do what no other power can do."

What about you? Are you sensing God leading you to conquer a humanly "impossible" challenge? Does it seem like all that was known to you before is now insurmountable in the shadow of looming mountains of uncertainties? God's words to Moses and the people of God, thousands of years ago, are the same to us today:

Crown of Beauty International

"The LORD Himself goes before you and will be with you. He will never leave you nor forsake you. Do not be afraid; do not be discouraged" (Deuteronomy 31:8).

It could be that what God is leading you to is even better than what you had expected or imagined. If God is with us, shall we then not go forth?

Today's Bible Reading: Deuteronomy 31:1-8
By Julie Branstetter

For Such a Time as This

YOU ARE NOT ALONE

One of the difficulties of going through a crisis is that we often feel alone in our suffering. Strength comes when we know that others are standing with us through our difficulties. Sisters and brothers, you are not alone. God is with us. The Lord will provide others to walk through the darkness with you. And you may be the one who is to encourage another by showing them that they are not alone. Is it enough to tell ourselves to be strong and courageous? That may be a temporary fix. What we really need is to know that God is with us, and that we can walk through this in community.

Let's see how Joshua led his community to walk through a challenging time to victory. He began by listening and hearing from God. The Lord said:

> "As I was with Moses, so I will be with you; I will never leave you nor forsake you. Be strong and courageous, because you will lead these people to inherit the land I swore to their forefathers to give

them. Be strong and very courageous" (Joshua 1:5-7).

Though we are not the Israelites wandering the desert and waiting to inherit the promised land, there is still truth in their story for us as we journey through crises. Notice Joshua's orders in verses 6-8. 1) Be strong and courageous, 2) Obey all the laws God has given you through Moses, 3) Meditate on the Book of the Law, day and night, 4) Lead the people to take the promised land.

These are good instructions for us. Though we do not need to lead people to the promised land, we can lead them to a place of hope by sharing God's promises. Encourage others by reminding them of God's faithfulness, loving presence, and sovereignty.

In 2 Corinthians 1:8-10, the apostle Paul revealed to the Corinthian church how their prayers were helping him and his coworkers through their intense suffering from persecution.

> "On Him we have set our hope that He will continue to deliver us, as you help us by your prayers. Then many will give thanks on our behalf for the gracious favor granted us in answer to the prayers of many" (2 Corinthians 1:8-10).

Do you see how our prayers can help those who are suffering? Seek the Lord as to the ways you can minister to others. Deliver food, care for an animal of a sick neighbor, give money to help those in need, call or email friends, family, or those who are all alone and struggling, and PRAY. These are all ways we minister God's love to others. You are not alone. Reach out and show others that they too are not alone!

I love how God closes His motivational speech to Joshua:

For Such a Time as This

"Have I not commanded you? Be strong and courageous. Do not be terrified; do not be discouraged, for the Lord your God will be with you wherever you go" (Joshua 1:9).

Sisters and brothers, do not be fearful or discouraged in difficult seasons. God is with you!

Today's Bible reading: Joshua 1:5-9; 2 Corinthians 1:3-11.
By Sue Corl

Crown of Beauty International

HOW WE RESPOND

Part II

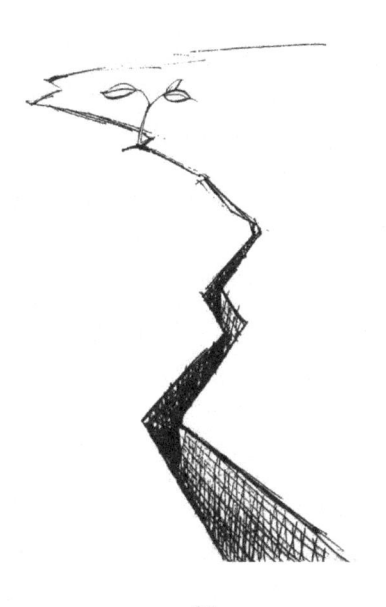

For Such a Time as This

HOW SHOULD WE
RESPOND TO BAD REPORTS?

Every day the world news is full of distressing events. If we listen for hours to the reports of tragedies, wars, corruption, and the negative impact on the world economy, we can become quite anxious or even depressed. One thing we could choose to do is to boycott the news. This may keep us in a false sense of security, but it will not enable us to be informed as to how our authorities want us to act or how to pray for the needs of the world.

So what should we do? How should we respond to bad reports? Look at the historical account in Deuteronomy 1:19-46 and Numbers 13-14 of a group of spies who were sent by their leader to check out the enemy territory.

God promised the Israelites that He would give them an abundant land full of milk and honey. They were to go against the enemies and conquer the land. The Lord told them not to be afraid or discouraged for He would be with them and enable them to be victorious. Out of caution, the people wanted to send spies to check out the land first. God agreed and twelve men were appointed. Ten of the spies came back admitting it was an abundant land. However, they followed this with terrifying reports of the power and size of the people, saying some were giants. They spoke of how well the cities were fortified.

> "'We can't attack those people; they are stronger than we are.' And they spread among the Israelites a bad report" (Numbers 13:31-32).

The people became stirred up and fearful. Two of the spies, Joshua and Caleb silenced the crowd and encouraged them that they would be able to take possession of the land.

> "If the Lord is pleased with us, He will lead us into that land, a land flowing with milk and honey, and will give it to us . . . the Lord is with us. Do not be afraid of them" (Numbers 14:8-9).

But the negative reports continued, and the people grumbled. They lost faith and hope. They became angry at God and accused Him of hating them (See Deuteronomy 1:26). They doubted God's intentions and goodness. Where did all this doubt come from? "Our brothers have made us lose heart" through their bad reports (Deuteronomy 1:28).

Do you see the power of discouraging words? Hopelessness and anxiety come when we look at our circumstances without seeking the Lord in prayer. As we pray to Him, rather than just reiterating the bad news to God, it is important to first take time to worship Him for His awesome character. Proclaim what the Word says about Him, then seek Him for understanding and peace. It was not wrong for the

For Such a Time as This

Israelites to take some time to check out the enemy they were up against. But in the face of fear, they needed to claim who God is and the promises He had given them. He promised them victory.

As we look first at the character of God and all the many truths about adversity, we will have hope that comes from knowing that God is in control. He is greater than our enemy (even our silent enemy). He desires us to be engaged in the battle through prayer. Take up your shield of faith, the sword of the Spirit and the Word, and pray.

Today's Bible Reading: Deuteronomy 1:19-46 and
Numbers 13-14
By Sue Corl

THOUGH I WALK
THROUGH THE VALLEY

"Even though I walk through the valley of the shadow of death, I will fear no evil, for you are with me; your rod and your staff, they comfort me"
(Psalm 23:4).

What a declaration of faith from the mouth of David, a man familiar with hardships and the emotional strain lurking in their midst. Though this verse from Psalm 23 is one we are likely all familiar with, I invite you to glean with me from the words of the psalmist, as you invite the Holy Spirit to speak and offer counsel to your heart.

As I read Psalm 23, my eyes were drawn to verse four (see above). However, the more I sat in the verse, the more evident it became that David was only able to make this declaration of faith because he was standing on God's promises and truths. His song starts with a declaration of who the Lord is, followed by what that means in his life: "The LORD is my shepherd; I shall not want" (verse 1). David was very familiar with the role of a shepherd, having been one as a boy. He knew the great cost and sacrifice the Shepherd would go to for the protection and care of his sheep, this being the Shepherd's greatest priority and joy.

As you read Psalm 23, don't miss the simple yet profound truth, friends, that the LORD your personal Shepherd. Take a moment to remind your soul of who your God is. Speak out the names of God that you know. Bring to mind the Hebrew Old Testament names that the Lord uses for Himself. He is Jehovah Jireh (my provider), Jehovah Rophe (my healer), Jehovah Nissi (my banner), and El Shaddai (my supplier). There are many others as well. He is your personal Shepherd, the Lord God Almighty. He is walking with you and will supply all that you need. He has promised this to you.

David then continues in verses two and three: "He makes me lie down in green pastures. He leads me beside still waters. He restores my soul. He leads me in paths of righteousness for His name's sake." The Lord Jesus is inviting your soul to find rest in Him. Sit in these two verses for a few moments and ask the Holy Spirit to usher you into a place of green pastures and still, calm waters. Allow Him to identify and personally invite you to trade the thoughts and concerns that are troubling you for His rest. Turn your attention away from where the world is leading you, in fear and confusion, and turn your face towards your Shepherd who is leading you in truth and peace.

Let us bring our attention back to verse four (see above). Notice David's recognition here that there will be times of trouble. There will be valleys where fear of evil will be waiting to overtake you. I think it is safe to say, the temptation to cower in fear has likely touched us all. Are you able to say in your heart, like David, that you will fear no evil, for the Lord your God is with you? Are you able to shift your perspective from fear and chaos and look at the Lord's rod and staff guiding you and offering comfort in His near presence? If you are, take this time to offer praise to the Lord your God and keep your eyes fixed upon Him. If you're not, know that the Holy Spirit longs to provide this peace and assurance in your heart. Allow Him to do it. Remember, David was able to say he would fear no evil only because he knew the One who was walking with him, the One who had led him through many trials before, the One who was guiding him, who would never forsake him or leave him alone. This same One is walking with you now.

Today's Bible Reading: Psalm 23.
By Nancy Martin

For Such a Time as This

AN ENCOUNTER WITH JESUS
The Testimony of a Valuable Daughter, Nancy Martin

As I laid prostrate across my bedroom floor, I became overwhelmed by the feeling that I had to get lower before the Lord. It was as if a weight of shame were crushing me, while the floorboards prevented me from lowering myself further. How did I get here? How did this happen? How do I tell anyone? What do I do now? God please - help me.

Growing up as a middle child provided many rich blessings in my life, yet unfortunately, comparison became familiar from a young age and began to color the years that followed. I used to joke that the intellectual abilities, musical talents, and really "the brains" were passed down to my older sister, skipped over me, and landed on my younger brother. I watched them succeed with what looked like minimal effort in comparison to the hard work, necessary help, and many more tries I felt I had to take.

Despite my mom's kind and godly reminders of how special God has made me and the gifts He has uniquely bestowed upon me – it never felt like enough. During my Middle School years leading into the beginning of High School, I began to struggle with my weight which added to these feelings of inferiority and insignificance. Without realizing it, I began striving for the approval and acceptance of others – longing for it, as if my value, my worth, and significance were dependent upon them.

As an intentional follower of Jesus, my fellow classmates knew I was a Christian and I had no problem being "different" in that way. But feeling different with my more reserved personality and inability to understand things as promptly as my friends wasn't a difference I wanted to have. By the end of High School, I was seeped deep in a lie that my personal worth was contingent much less upon who I was but rather upon what I could do and how well I could do it.

Naturally, this didn't go away simply because I started attending a Christian University, in fact, that lie became even louder and more suggestive. When college men began to pursue me, my hungry heart, crying out for acceptance and significance, led me into friendships and relationships that were anything but a good fit. I was getting the attention I had craved for so long, was being pursued and wanted by men, and felt accepted (if I acted a certain way). But I couldn't shake off the feelings of disappointment, disgust, dissatisfaction, and shame. Something wasn't right; it didn't feel like this was who I really was, as if I were wearing a mask that I didn't know how to take off.

So there I was, about to graduate, lying prostrate across my bedroom floor, overwhelmed by the feeling that I must get lower before the Lord, it was as if a weight of shame was crushing me, while the floorboards prevented me from lowering myself further. How did I get here? How did this happen? How do I tell anyone? What do I do now? God please - help me. It was here that the Lord began to answer those questions and open my eyes in new ways to truth.

The Holy Spirit met my ready heart and began to show me how the lie I believed, that I was inferior, not good enough, and unacceptable, had led me to this place of comparison, of looking to others, and at that time, looking to men, to fill the longings in my heart to be wanted and accepted for exactly who I was. I didn't want to have to be "good enough". I just wanted to be Nancy; I wanted that to be enough. Once I could see that, God began to show me through His Word that my value and my worth were never meant to be found in others. They were only ever meant to be found in Him. The longings I had in my heart could only first and foremost be satisfied in the One who created those longings to be satisfied

For Such a Time as This

by Him. It was as if I was the woman at the well in John 4; though our stories are completely different, Jesus was meeting me in my hurt, my disappointment, and my shame. He was offering me the living water (true words of healing) I had been searching for. This ignited a greater hunger to grow in truth.

I began connecting with Sue Corl, founder, and director of Crown of Beauty International, and began studying the Crown of Beauty Bible Study. Within that study, truth became more personal to my life and story than it ever had been before. There is so much more growth the Lord has in store for me, this I know for sure, but His Word proves true in my life; "Then you will know the truth, and the truth will set you free" (John 8:32).

RUN TO THE FATHER

There is a beautiful song called Run to the Father, by Cody Carnes. You will be greatly encouraged if you listen to it. These are the words:

> "I've carried a burden for too long on my own.
> I wasn't created to bear it alone.
> I hear Your invitation to let it all go.
> Yeah, I see it now. I'm laying it down.
> And I know that I need You.
> I run to the Father. I fall into grace.
> I'm done with the hiding. No reason to wait.
> My heart needs a surgeon. My soul needs a friend.
> So I'll run to the Father,
> again and again, and again, and again.
> You saw my condition. Had a plan from the start.
> Your Son for redemption. The price for my heart.
> I don't have a context for that kind of love.

For Such a Time as This

I don't understand. I can't comprehend.
All I know is I need You."

In difficult times of uncertainty, we will find hope when we run to the Father who is unchanging. Three things that never change are the character of God, our identity in Christ, and His promises. No matter what our circumstances, God's nature never changes. The first time that God described himself was to Moses. "Then the Lord came down in the cloud and stood there with Moses and proclaimed his name, the Lord. And he passed in front of Moses, proclaiming, "The Lord, the Lord, the compassionate and gracious God, slow to anger, abounding in love and faithfulness, maintaining love to thousands, and forgiving wickedness, rebellion, and sin" (Exodus 34:5-7a).

Our Father is so patient. He sent us prophets and priests to tell us how we should live. When we still did not listen, He sent His Son. Jesus taught us the way we should live to bring honor and love to God and to our neighbors. But still, we did not and do not listen. We rebel. We live our lives in pride, independent of God. We do things our way, rather than seeking God's way. We cling to man-made idols (like money) to find comfort, hope, peace, and pride. Too often, we selfishly seek these out to please ourselves or our family members but ignore the needy around us.

We must also realize that God is a righteous judge who will punish rebellion and idolatry. However, God pours out His grace upon us. Though we deserve punishment, God sent His own Son to bear the punishment for us. The Lord gives us a choice to turn away from self-absorption and idolatry. When we turn to follow Christ and receive His gracious provision for our sins, He will lead us out of darkness into light. These are dark times for people all around the world. The Lord calls us to pray for His mercy. To pray for people to turn away from self and idols and turn to Jesus. He is the Shepherd who can lead us out of the storm, away from the enemies that want to destroy our bodies and souls.

Amidst great trials and persecution, the Psalmists call us to look to the Father from whom comes our help. All of Psalm 46 assures us that if we look to God, our fear will go, and our help will come. Lift our eyes up to the Maker of heaven and earth from whom comes our help (see Psalm 121:1-2). The apostle John tells us of the Father's great love for us. "How great is the love the Father has lavished on us, that we should be called children of God" (1 John 3:1). God reaches out to us, understanding our fears. He knows we struggle to trust Him during times of uncertainty. Where will our food come from? Will I have any money a month from now? Will my family stay healthy? Will those I know and love who are sick get better? God calls us to pray and ask (see Matthew 7:7). He also tells us not to worry because our Father knows all our needs. Take advantage of our privileged inheritance and run to our Father with all your needs (see Matthew 6:25-33). God is unchanging. Our identity is unchanging. God's promises are unchanging. Trust me when I say, things are not as uncertain as they seem.

Today's Bible Reading: Exodus 34:5-7; Matthew 6:25-33
By Sue Corl

For Such a Time as This

AM I LAVISH WITH JESUS?

As I write this morning, I am aware of this unusual time of relative isolation, on-line meetings, and ever-changing news, I have struggled off and on to focus during my quiet times with the Lord. My mind seems to wander more easily, and I find it hard to organize my thoughts and day. Thankfully, I am not alone! I'm so thankful that Jesus cherishes every effort I take to be close to Him and to give Him first place throughout my day. I'm especially encouraged by the stories of others who gave to Jesus out of their lack.

Mark 14 gives an account of Jesus being anointed with oil by a sinful woman as He visited a prominent man in Bethany. The costly oil she used represented her life savings and/or her dowry for a future marriage proposal. She considered this offering of "all that she had" worth the expense. Jesus comments in verse 8 that "she did what she could." Her sacrifice was worth making in exchange for the Savior's joy. At another time, Jesus observed a widow at the Temple putting in "all that she had" (See Mark 12:41-44). This story is similar to the story of the woman in Mark 14, for the poor widow also offered to God everything she had in her meager reserves, trusting that He would care for all her needs.

Both stories raise a question: Am I lavish with Jesus? What does it mean for me to be generous with my Lord? Below are a few ways I believe God intends to grow us in generosity toward Him:

First, I can be generous with my time and attention upon Jesus. Another way to say this is: I am allowed to "waste" time with Jesus! If I struggle to remain attentive to Christ, especially in times of financial hardship or social isolation, He promises to help me.

> "Jesus knows we're like sheep that, once they are on their backs, are helpless to roll over by themselves. Our Shepherd understands our helplessness and will surprise us with His ready response. He has an abundance of ways to encourage us to be faithful… Rely on His faithfulness to help you, not on your own faithfulness to always do your best." [Aletha Hinthon, How to Read the Bible So It Changes Your Life]

Next, I can be lavish in my acceptance and patience with others. I can slow down and be present in the moment with the ones He has placed in front of me. I can practice selflessness as I serve my family, colleagues, roommates, and friends with a willing spirit. Psalm 51:12 is a prayer we can pray for renewed desire.

> "Restore to me the joy of Your salvation and grant me a willing spirit, to sustain me."

Jesus takes delight in our willingness to do His will,

For Such a Time as This

whether it is listening, encouraging, serving behind the scenes, or quietly praying for others.

Finally, I can be generous because I trust Him for provision.

> "The LORD…who satisfies your desires with good things so that your youth is renewed like the eagle's" (Psalm 103:5).

"Provision" also includes my social, emotional, and spiritual well-being. When I trust Him to be my Provider, I can be generous with others who seem needier than myself, knowing He will meet my every need.

Perhaps in this season of waiting, we can ask the Lord what "she did what she could" means for each of us. He sees the limitations of our reserves, so being lavish with Jesus may look different for each of us. May His Spirit lead you as you offer Him your attentiveness and obedience.

Today's Bible Reading: Mark 12:41-44; 14:3-9.
By Julie Branstetter

SOLID ROCK OR BEDROCK?

When I was a kid, my sister, one of our dear friends, and I were exploring the woods near our friend's home. We came across a patch of green moss we all thought had overgrown, covering the solid earth beneath it. Together, the three of us stepped onto the moss and instantly sunk into a swamp. Needless to say, we walked home that day wet, dirty, and dreading the unforeseen consequences. To this day, that experience is still etched in my mind. The mossy patch looked so solid but wow, did it surprise us!

I think we've all experienced surprise and disappointment at times because of a "solid foundation" falling through. Daily, the world bombards us with messages trying to convince us of what foundations we should stand on. None follow through on the promise of security and peace we so desperately seek. During crises, those foundations start to feel shaky and unsure. I think it is times like these where God graciously allows us to recognize some of the worldly foundations we have been standing on. We then have a choice: to repent and rebuild or remain and wait.

This reminds me of a familiar parable. Let us look at Matthew 7:24-27 (ESV) together:

> "Everyone then who hears these words of mine and does them will be like a wise man who built his house on the rock. And the rain fell, and the floods came, and the winds blew and beat on that house, but it did not fall, because it had been founded on the rock. And everyone who hears these words of mine and does not do them will be like a foolish man who built his house on the sand. And the rain fell, and the floods came, and the winds blew and beat against that house, and it fell, and great was the fall of it."

My ESV Study Bible gave a helpful analysis of Jesus' parable. This parable brings Jesus' Sermon on the Mount to a close (Matthew 5-7). Jesus is calling his listeners to make a choice. Are they going to choose Jesus or the religious establishment of their day? He is drawing a line between Himself and any other foundation established by a group or culture. He identifies Himself as distinct, set apart from all others. To quote the ESV Study Commentary, "Disciples who build their lives on the bedrock of Jesus and His message of the kingdom of heaven are truly wise, regardless of the shifting cultural or religious fashions [governments]" (Matthew 7:24-27; page 1834). Webster's Dictionary defines bedrock as, "1: the solid rock underlying unconsolidated surface materials (such as soil) 2a: lowest point b: basis ("the bottom of something considered as its foundation").

During the time in which Jesus spoke this parable, His listeners likely knew that within the summer months, the sand that was near the Sea of Galilee was hard because of the sun and heat. A wise builder however would know that when the seasons changed, the hard surface would soften and once the rains or floods hit, the structure built upon that rock would fall. The wise builder would dig several feet below the hard summer surface until he hit the bedrock. Once the bedrock was exposed, the foundation could then be built. Only then would it remain sturdy against the destructive rains and floods - no matter the season.

I wonder how often we build on the hard surface, rather than digging deeper to reach the bedrock. Have there been times throughout these trying few months where your foundations were shaken?

To any of us who can relate to fear or distress from our circumstances, it is time to start digging deeper. It is time to dig deeper into the Scriptures for your own study, knowledge, and application from the Holy Spirit. It is time to press deeper into prayer, not only beseeching the Lord on behalf of our families, communities, country, and the world, but also repenting of the shaky foundations we have stood upon that were not Christ. Jesus has laid the foundation for us. Let us not be the foolish man who settled for the hard surface that seemed firm but when the trials and the storms of life came his house fell, "and great was the fall of it." Let us be like the wise man who built his foundation upon the bedrock...Jesus.

> "So this is what the Sovereign Lord says: "See, I lay a stone in Zion, a tested stone, a precious cornerstone for a sure foundation; the one who relies on it will never be stricken with panic" (Isaiah 28:16 NIV).

Today's Bible Reading: Matthew 7:24-27; Isaiah 28:16; 2 Timothy 2:15
By Nancy Martin

For Such a Time as This

AN ATTITUDE OF EXPECTANCY

"His sister stood at a distance to see what would happen to him" (Exodus 2:4).

Life is filled with uncertainty. If we let them, difficult circumstances can shake our foundation, especially if we have built our sense of security on the expectation that our world is stable. Nothing of this world is secure, but we can rely on God as our security. He goes beyond satisfying and exceeding our own expectations and desires. I know this on a day to day basis, but it is in moments of crisis that this truth is tested. As I have faced crises and uncertainties, I often find myself responding with fear and distrust of God's goodness. I become paralyzed, unable to move in trust that God is working a perfect plan for my life. It is in these moments that I am reminded of Miriam, a child herself, watching Moses in the river to see "what would happen to him" (Exodus 2:4). If you have the time, open your Bible now, and read Exodus 2:1-10.

"His sister stood at a distance to see what would happen to him" (Exodus 2:4).

This simple sentence says a lot about Miriam's relationship with God. She had limitations in her stance; all she could do was watch and see what would happen to Moses. If she took him back out of the river, Moses would be just as unsafe among his family as he was among the Nile. So Miriam stands, waiting for God to act. In our own lives, we face similar limitations in our circumstances. We can take matters into our own hands, but this can only take us so far. I have faced limitations as I have moved across the country, trying to juggle securing an apartment and job. In fact, I lost my housing a week before moving, and all I could do was trust and expect that God would provide. It has been a continuous effort to prevent myself from trying to plan and figure it out on my own. When I failed to trust God over the last few weeks, I have been reminded of Miriam standing at the Nile, knowing all she could do was watch and take on an attitude of expectancy knowing that Moses' fate was in God's hands.

This attitude does not only fill us with the peace that surpasses all understanding, but it also prepares us to respond when God makes a way. We see this in Miriam's bold and daring response to the Pharaoh's daughter; "Shall I go and get one of the Hebrew women to nurse the baby for you?" (Exodus 2:7). Miriam had such a tense anticipation of God's hand in her circumstances that she was able to act with courage. I want the same boldness and anticipation; I want to be expectant! It is easy to fall into discouragement and fear, and there is no shame in slipping up, but I encourage you to not stay there. Be expectant of what God is going to do!

God often exceeds our expectations and desires. I assume that when Moses' mother and Miriam put him in the Nile, their greatest desire was that he would live. They did not ex-

For Such a Time as This

pect to have him brought back to them for his toddler years, or that his mother would be paid to nurse him, or that he would be raised as Egyptian royalty(Exodus 2:9-10). I believe God's plan for us is always better than what we hoped for.. We need to be expectant no matter what our circumstances are. Even though we may find ourselves nearsighted and unable to imagine a way out, let us choose to expect the unexpected from our Lord and Savior who knows our hearts better than we know them.

Today's Bible Reading: Exodus 2:1-10
By Kaelah Byrom

THE REWARDER OF THOSE
WHO SEEK HIM

"And without faith it is impossible to please God, because anyone who comes to Him must believe that He exists and that He rewards those who earnestly seek Him" (Hebrews 11:6).

Most of us would say that we desire to please God, but the questions to ask ourselves are: How much do we desire to please God, and how do we go about doing this?

The apostle Paul said that it was his life ambition to please God. His passion was to bring delight to the Lord. He felt there was no sacrifice too great to make for the Savior. He considered all his worldly accomplishments rubbish so that He could "gain Christ" (see Philippians 3:7-9). Paul is not to be the exception. We are exhorted to be imitators of Paul because he was living his life in a Christ-like manner for the glory of God. Is our desire to please God above all else? This is what the Lord asks of us. Living this kind of life requires surrender and sacrifice, but it also brings great reward. Only when we die to ourselves, to bring glory to God, can we fully experience the abundant life that Christ promised.

So, how do we go about pleasing God? We are told in Hebrews 11:6 that we must have faith. In fact, the writer emphasizes that it is IMPOSSIBLE to please God without faith. As I began my morning today by praying through my week, I could feel the tension in my spirit rising. I sensed the Lord asking me if I had a heart of faith. If I am anxious, am I doubting that God will give me the strength and ability to handle all that He brings to my day? It was Paul's faith in the character of God that enabled him to say that he can do everything through Christ who gives him strength (see Philippians 4:13). It was this same faith that allowed him to be content in whatever circumstances he had to bear (see 4:11-12).

It is not enough just to do good works to please the Lord. He wants us to do them by faith in His Spirit's power and His provision. When we begin to focus on our own abilities and wisdom, we are moving away from faith and toward our flesh. The result will be the fruit of the flesh, rather than the fruit of the Spirit. If you are anxious about something, ask the Lord to fill you with faith to believe that He will provide for you, and strengthen you each day.

As you continue to wait for life to begin to feel more "normal" again, how is the condition of your faith? Has it been dwindling as your difficult circumstances continue? Is it feeling like a roller coaster at times, soaring up some days and down other days? If you are being honest with yourself, do you see your faith steadfast in God alone, or placed also in others, or your own abilities to stay "safe?" Though it is good for us to be aware of what is going on and make wise, daily decisions to deal with the difficulties we face, our hope is to remain ultimately in the Lord. May you seek Him today and allow Him to reveal to you the current condition of your faith. I pray we receive an even greater outpouring of faith from the heart of God into our own hearts.

Today's Bible Reading: Hebrews 11:6, Philippians 3-4:1
By Sue Corl and Nancy Martin

For Such a Time as This

WHAT IS IT?

Exodus chapter 16 - talk about a crazy time to be alive! The Israelites had recently witnessed God's mighty hand against their oppressors, the Egyptians. Ten plagues had ravaged through their enemy's land. They watched the Red Sea literally part before their eyes and safely walked through on the dry ground, only to see it come crashing down upon their pursuing captors. And now they find themselves journeying through the desert. They're not sure what will happen next. There is no doubt that they found themselves asking how long they will be there, where their food and water will come from, or what will happen to them once they get to the land the Lord had promised them.

Those unsettling thoughts and questions might sound familiar to you right now. Perhaps your life seems very uncertain. How long will this trial last? What will happen in my future? Will I have enough money? Will those I love remain healthy? Is my job stable? What will the economy be like in the future? And if you're anything like me, when you go through crises, you find yourself often saying, "What day is it today?" You are not the only one asking these sorts of questions. But there is much we can learn from the story of Exodus 16 about our own hearts and how we respond to trials and difficulties.

The chapter begins with a very pressing need. The people are hungry and they have no food. So they begin to complain to Moses and Aaron (their leaders). Whether out of hunger, emotional distress, or both, they even start to say crazy things like: "...Would that we had died by the hand of the LORD in the land of Egypt, when we sat by the meat pots and ate bread to the full, for you have brought us out into this wilderness to kill this whole assembly with hunger" (16:3).

Despite their wayward attitudes, the Lord hears their grumblings and so He responds: "Then the LORD said to Moses, 'Behold, I am about to rain bread from heaven for you, and the people shall go out and gather a day's portion every day, that I may test them, whether they will walk in my law or not'" (16:4). Moses and Aaron relayed the Lord's message to the people, making sure they heard each word and command the Lord had spoken.

Sure enough, just as the Lord had promised, "In the evening quail came up and covered the camp, and in the morning, dew lay around the camp. And when the dew had gone up, there was on the face of the wilderness a fine, flake-like thing, fine as frost on the ground ["manna"]. When the people of Israel saw it, they said to one another, 'What is it?' For they did not know what it was. And Moses said to them, 'It is the bread that the LORD has given you to eat.'" (Exodus 16:13-15).

I love the people's initial response to the Lord's provision of manna, "What is it?" Have you ever received provision from the Lord and not recognized it at first because it wasn't something familiar? Or maybe it wasn't what you were expecting, or what you thought God's response should have been? Or perhaps the overwhelming voices of fear and doubt around you hindered your own sight. I wonder how often we continue grumbling or feeling anxious, even in the midst of God's grace and provision toward us, because we're unable to recognize it, even when it's right in front of us.

As I considered the Israelites' predicament, this thought struck me; the people could have spent the night in their tents full of anxious thoughts about tomorrow even though God had provided for them just that day. It would have been easy to stay up all night fretting over the next meal, worried that there wouldn't be food. Maybe their conversations repeatedly circled back to overwhelming questions. Will we have food tomorrow? What will tomorrow have in store for us? They likely felt uncertain at times. I would suggest that God knew exactly what He was doing by having the people take just enough manna for the day. He knew if the people were to daily trust Him, this test of faith would reveal the condition of their hearts. They could choose anxiety or trust, fear or faith. Just like God provided for His people in the desert, He will provide for you now. My ongoing prayer for you is that you will have eyes to see the daily manna the Lord is pouring out. May you daily trust and obey Jehovah Jireh.

Today's Bible Reading: Exodus 16; John 6:30-35;
Matthew 6:25-34
By Nancy Martin

RUNNING AIMLESSLY
OR RUNNING WELL

Hebrews 11 is often known as the "Hall of Faith." The writer recalls the heroic saints who journeyed before us, having demonstrated unwavering faith in God despite the hardships and tribulations these heroes encountered along the way. At the beginning of Hebrews 12, we are told why the writer has championed their stories. As we learn of their deep faith and great works for the kingdom, we are motivated to turn away from the things that keep us from steadfastly walking with God. Taking this verse apart piece by piece gives us a picture of a race.

Here we are at the starting line preparing to run. The stands are full of godly men and women like Noah, Abraham, Rahab, and Joseph, who are cheering us on! They are smiling, clapping, and calling out to us: "You can do this! Don't give up! Keep looking forward!" They have already run the race and finished to win the prize. Paul, who plays the role of sports commentator in this image, cries out: "Do you not know that in a race all the runners run, but only one gets the prize? Run in such a way as to get the prize" (1 Corinthians 9:24). You turn and see this man full of joy and contentment. You quickly are reminded of his journey on earth where he relentlessly kept going and preaching the gospel no matter how difficult things became. You recall his astounding words that he wrote while in prison.

For I have learned to be content whatever the circumstances. I know what it is to be in need, and I know what it is to have plenty. I have learned the secret of being content in any and every situation, whether well fed or hungry, whether living in plenty or in want. I can do everything through him who gives me strength (Philippians 4:11-13).

His words calm your anxiety and a surge of energy fills your body. You find yourself starting to chant the words from the fans: "You can do this! You can do this!" Suddenly the Holy Spirit interrupts your thoughts and turns your attention to the deep voice of the prophet Zechariah. "'Not by might nor by power, but by my Spirit' says the Lord Almighty" (Zechariah 4:6). Immediately you confess that you were about to take on this race in your own strength, and repentantly you ask the Spirit to fill you with His power and wisdom. Now you are ready. You have been training hard. You still have a long way to go to be as faithful as the saints who are cheering you on, but you are willing to take on this next challenge.

The gun goes off and with every muscle, you push off from the starting block. After you stand up, you begin to pump your arms. You notice a couple of runners ahead of you. Anxiously, you begin to pump your arms even harder, but you forget what your coaches have told you about the proper positioning of your arms. You go back to your old way of running, and you notice other runners begin to pass you. This only causes you even greater anxiety, and you put your head down and push even harder. Your coach, the Holy Spirit, abruptly breaks into your concentration and reminds you of the words of the apostle Paul: "Therefore, I do not run like a man running aimlessly" (1 Corinthians 9:26). You remember the coaching you were given about your posture as you run. Your arms straighten out, your head goes up, and your speed immediately increases. You notice a runner falls behind you. Then another. And another. You thank God that His ways are always the best. Our own ways and following the teaching of the world is folly. Now you are in a beautiful stride. You ask the Lord to help you continue in His strength and His ways.

Take some time today to stop and ask the Lord whose voice you are listening to as you run your daily race. Are you listening to the Holy Spirit and the words of the saints who wrote the Holy Bible? Are you turning back to your old ways of doing things? Are you letting fear or anxious thoughts sweep back in, or are you standing firm on the Rock that is unshakable? Are you giving up on what the Lord has purposed for you to do right now because you feel tired and "over it?" The Holy Spirit will help you keep running. If you have stopped, confess this to the Lord. Ask Him to link arms with you and get you back up and going. Let us run in such a way as to get the prize.

Today's Bible Reading: Hebrews 12:1;
1 Corinthians 9:24-27; Zechariah 4:6
By Sue Corl and Nancy Martin

For Such a Time as This

FREED FROM PERFECTIONISM INTO GRACE
Julie Branstetter's Testimony

For many years, grace was a nebulous concept to me. Born with a strong-willed, conscientious personality, I tended to rely on personal strengths, talents or discipline to achieve the "results" I wanted in life. Ambition carried me for several years. I felt I could resolve any difficulty through good planning and hard work; I believed knowing the right interpersonal skills would keep me from facing conflict. My achievements since childhood had proven that!

Although I loved Jesus since childhood, I never seemed to be able to break through from "perfectionist" determination to a place of divine rest. I gained ground in seeing myself the way God sees me, but in reality, I was living on the see-saw of one foot on salvation by grace and one foot on salvation by works. There was definitely progress as I leaned into the Lord and studied His Word, as well as immersed myself in worshipping in His presence, but I still tended to fall back into self-effort.

I remember a couple of instances in my early adult years when I needed to relinquish a job role that I felt I was good at and defined my value as a minister. In the first instance, I was giving up my right to do what I loved in the church (leading music) to someone else who was more mature and well-suited for that role. I needed to surrender what I loved so I could do something that needed to be done—working with the youth of the church. Oh, how my pride and desire for appreciation had to die in that transition! In a second instance, for years I recruited and equipped teachers to work overseas in a hard place. I was grasping for recognition from others for a job well done. Without even saying something about my internal struggle, the spiritual sister who was assuming my job sent me a timely message reminding me not to place my value in what I DO, but in who I AM to my Father. That was another humbling experience!

It wasn't until my late 30's that Jesus helped me to break through to total freedom with Him and to be done, once and for all, with a "works-based" acceptance.

Our family went through a couple of years of home-schooling my child who has a neurological condition and learning disabilities, and healing from a family crisis. To add on to that, I also was recovering from a physical and mental breakdown. In this season the Lord finally broke the last remnant of the "perfectionist" in me. After I had exhausted everything—my health, relationships, and my child's development— I truly felt like giving up. I remember boarding a public bus just to clear my head and try to figure out what had gone wrong. It was in that moment that the Lord came and spoke very clearly to my heart: "So you see, all that is left is Grace." I could sense His invitation to fall back into His loving, open arms. I returned home with newfound understanding and hope. This was, He revealed, His never-failing mercy and gracious restoration—when I had failed at all I thought I was good at. At the end of my rope, there was Jesus.

There have been other miraculous breakthroughs in my life as well: receiving instantaneous emotional healing from the bondage of huge losses and wounds of the past, gradual deliverance from a cycle of depression, miraculous protection and provision when our daughters were hit by a car and hospitalized for eight days, and divine healing from a progressive eye disease. I should be half-blind, but on Good Friday God touched me in response to His promise that He would heal me! These are all signs of His touch on my life.

I'm grateful for every part of the journey, because those

For Such a Time as This

scars are signs of HIS Grace. I am able to guide others into freedom because I have also been set free! All of these experiences have served as reminders of who He is and what He can do. His heart is for me, not against me! He is the God of "more than enough" and of "exceeding, abundantly above all we could ask, think or imagine." To Him be the Glory for this redeemed life!

ASK FOR GOD-GIVEN DREAMS

"Hope deferred makes the heart sick, but a dream fulfilled is a tree of life" (Proverbs 13:12).

Unfortunately, when tragedy, pandemics, or other unexpected difficulties come our way, our plans change, and things we were looking forward to are canceled. When something very important to us keeps getting put off, our heart sinks. We wait. We hope. We pray. But nothing changes. Even our God-given dreams can get delayed month after month. Personally, I have had five trips and seven conferences canceled that I was very excited about. When each one gets postponed, my spirit groans.

But the Lord says that a dream fulfilled is a tree of life. When I began to realize that a large part of my ministry could not happen for at least nine months, I asked the Holy Spirit to give me new dreams. He obviously knew that all the troubles going on in the world would affect travel plans and other significant events. But He wants to continue to work in and through our lives.

I asked the Lord to give me new dreams. God-given dreams bring life to us and others. He began to unfold His plans for the focus He wants me to have for the rest of the year. Little by little, as I pray, He is also revealing the details of this new dream.

> "The Lord directs the steps of the godly. He delights in every detail of their lives. Though they stumble, they will never fall, for the Lord upholds them by His hand" (Psalm 37:23-24 NLT).

Though at times I feel a bit sad that I will not see my dear friends in other countries, the Lord is comforting my heart. We can bring our disappointments to Him. He understands and He cares. If you are struggling with the question "Why Lord?", that is okay too. Bring it to Him. He wants to comfort the heart that is "sick." But as you continue to seek Him, He also wants to give you new dreams and hope for tomorrow.

God promises to guide your every action as you take steps to achieve His will. The catch is to seek God's dreams for you, not your own dreams. He knows you better than you know yourself, and He wired you from conception to live out His will. You can trust that His plans will bring you a satisfying and fulfilling life.

Here is an application step for you. This week pray every day for God to show you your next steps. What are the God-given dreams He has for you for the days, months, and possibly year ahead? Ask a close friend or family member who knows you well to pray for you. As things come to your mind, talk to this person about it. See if she/he brings confirmation to what you sense God is telling you. Spend time in the Word to allow Him to use Scripture during your time of seeking. As new dreams come, begin to take steps toward them.

"For I know the plans I have for you," says the Lord. "They are plans for good and not for disaster, to give you a future and a hope" (Jeremiah 29:11 NLT).

Today's Bible Reading: Proverbs 13:12 and Jeremiah 29:11
By Sue Corl and Doug Kozub

For Such a Time as This

HOW GOD RESPONDS

Part III

DON'T YOU CARE

Some weeks are more overwhelming than others. When physical and emotional strains build up with relentless weight and volume, we either tend to shut down, meltdown—or both! It is at these times that it is important to pour out praise and petitions to the One who can help. It is also critical that we cling to truth, so our hearts do not grow bitter and cordoned off from love.

This week I struggled to keep my head above water through multiple challenges. By going to the Father for His solution, He reminded me that our fallen nature tends to try and handle everything on its own. Then if we fail, we blame Him for our personal struggle or lack of faith. Jesus' disciples were no different.

When Jesus and the disciples sought to get away from the crowds, they encountered a storm in their small boat. The Scriptures say that the storm they encountered was "furious," such that the boat was nearly swamped. Jesus, being tired from ministry, was asleep in the boat on a cushion. The exasperated disciples ran to Him with this complaint: "Teacher, don't you care that we drown?" (Mark 4:38b). If we were to break down what the disciples were truly saying, it would sound like this: "Teacher, don't you care that we're about to die?" What an extreme accusation — "don't you care!" Did they know the Lord of heaven and earth—the great I AM—was in the boat with them that day? Apparently not yet.

Martha made the same accusation of Jesus when He and His disciples came to visit. Martha, being the older sister and the hostess, felt it was her responsibility to provide all the culturally expected gestures of a good hostess. She wanted to do her best for Jesus by not giving him and his disciples sub-average hospitality. But when she could no longer make herself or those around her rise to her own expectations, she blamed Jesus for not caring. "But Martha was distracted by all the preparations that had to be made. She came to Him and asked, 'Lord, don't you care that my sister has left me to do the work by myself'" (Luke 10:40a). And then Martha proceeded to tell Jesus what He should do! "Tell her to help me!" (Luke 10:40b). Martha had yet to understand His unfailing love.

When we are overwhelmed or frustrated with many things at once, we tend to display the same attitude toward our Lord. "Lord, don't you care? Don't you care that my mother is sick? Lord, don't you care that I've lost work and have no paycheck right now? Lord, don't you care that there is so much violence and injustice happening in the world?" To the doubting soul, that question remains; DOES He care?

Mary knew how to find the answer to this question. Through being still before Him and listening to His words, she began to recognize His heart. This simple exercise has helped me when I feel overwhelmed. As I sit before Jesus, I allow Him to show me all the things that I am overly worried about. I repent of an attitude that claims He doesn't care. And then in my journal after every item of concern, I write in ALL-CAPS the name JESUS! In doing so, I place the matter in His hands. I acknowledge the authority of His name. I surrender to His sovereign will and power at work in every situation, large or small. I acknowledge my own inability to do anything that will make lasting change. And I speak to my own soul, reminding myself to once more turn to Him with my whole being in total adoration. In doing so, I lean into His grace, trusting the situation and my response to Him.

May you find His sweet embrace at the end of your pen, at the end of your own efforts. As you reflect at the end of the day, may you say, "It is well with my soul."

Today's Bible Reading: Mark 4:36-41; Luke 10:38-42
By Julie Bransetter

For Such a Time as This

REVELING IN HIS CREATION

When difficulties come, instinctively we ask, "Why is this happening?" Several times in the Bible, God's people questioned Him as to why they were experiencing hardship. In many cases, God responded by pointing them to His great power demonstrated in creation. The Lord did not punish them for their questioning, but He drew their focus to ponder His Almighty nature.

We will bring our attention to the interactions Job had with God. Much of this lengthy book includes the numerous accusations that his friends made of Job. Over and over, they insisted that the great losses of family members, possessions, and good health must have been a result of God's punishment for Job's sin. Trial after trial came his way. Yet, Job continued to honor God by not turning away or accusing God of wrongdoing. We see Job defend himself declaring that he lived a righteous life. In fact, Job 26-31 is Job's discourse describing his exemplary behavior. I encourage you to read these chapters as they are a good guide as to how to live a godly life. Near the end of his prayer, he says, "I sign now my defense – let the Almighty answer me; let my accuser put his indictment in writing. Surely, I would wear it on my shoulder, I would put it on a crown. I would give him an account of my every step; like a prince I would approach him" (Job 31:35-37).

The Lord answers Job's request and responds with a long speech describing His great might and sovereignty over all creation. In Job 38-41, God answers Job by asking the question if he or any other human could create such an amazingly complex creation. He points out that the brilliant stars and the worshipful angels sing of His grandeur. The rolling waves, no man can stop. No one comprehends the vast expanse of the earth and the depths of the sea. God is sovereign over the lightning, the rain, and the snow. The weather must respond to His beckoning call. Only God can bring forth the constellations. Only He has dominion over the earth. Only God can create living creatures that have wisdom and understanding. It is God who put instincts in animals so they will hunt for their prey and run from danger. In each of His animals, He placed unique behavioral characteristics that enable them to reproduce, flourish, and adapt to the environments for which He placed them. The Lord drew Job's attention to the distinctive features of the mountain goats, bears, wild donkeys, wild oxen, ostriches, storks, horses, hawks, eagles, and two of the Lord's most powerful creatures at that time: the behemoths and the leviathans.

The Lord asks Job for a response: "Will the one who contends with the Almighty correct him? Let him who accuses God answer him!" (Job 40:1). Job was greatly humbled by his encounter with God. "I am unworthy – how can I reply to You? I put my hand over my mouth. I spoke once, but I have no answer – twice, but I will say no more" (Job 40:4-5). After God's boasting about the behemoth and the leviathan, Job's

For Such a Time as This

heart finally finds peace with God and declares, "I know that You can do all things; no plan of Yours can be thwarted . . . My ears have heard You but now my eyes have seen You" (Job 42:2, 4).

I will admit that Job is a difficult book to read. It is hard to understand why the Lord allowed Satan to bring such hardship upon Job. Sometimes it is puzzling why we or one we love is going through great suffering. However, I have found that when I am going through trials and pain, the Lord will deliver me out of darkness and into light when I focus on the Almighty's power and wisdom as revealed through His creation. The Lord helped Job to not "shrink God down to human size." He brought Job to see that the Lord is so much greater than our minds can conceive. His ways are not our ways. It is easy to question God's purposes, especially when we bring Him down to our human level. Thus, the Lord led Job to ponder the greatness of God's creation. I encourage you to frequently take walks and look at nature. If you have little nature near you, utilize the internet to view magnificent pictures of our universe. Ponder the complexity and vastness of God's creation. Praise Him for His great wisdom, power, and sovereignty. At times, use the name *Almighty* when you address Him. Like Job, this will help you to better acknowledge the wisdom of God and trust Him no matter what difficulties you are facing.

Today's Bible Reading: Job 26-31, 38-42.
By Sue Corl

HEALING FROM A TRAGEDY
Tyla Kozub's Testimony

As you get older you realize how many testimonies you have, but the one that I will never forget is when my brother passed away. As a young girl of 12 years old, soon to be 13, I loved being with my brother even though we fought a ton. As he started getting older, he would go out with his friends, and I would wish I could go with him. One day, He asked if I wanted to invite a friend and go to a beach park right outside Memphis, where we lived. I was so excited, that I organized it with my friend, I got permission from our parents, and off we went one beautiful Saturday midmorning.

After being at the park most of the day, my friend and I wanted to go home, but my brother was like "let's wait a little longer." Unbeknown to me, my brother and his friend had been drinking. I knew he was acting a little different, but I was too young to figure that out. On the way home, it started raining, and we hydroplaned off the road into a grassy field right into an electric pole. The car wrapped around the pole, throwing my brother out of the front window and leaving my friend and I in the back of the seat. The front seat was on top of our feet for two to three hours until the firefighters could cut us out.

A few days later, I remember waking up and thinking I heard a voice saying your brother is going to be fine. Now, at this point, my brother was in the hospital on a ventilator, brain dead. My parents had to make a hard decision of whether or not to take ing h him off the ventilator or not. Unfortunately, that afternoon we all went in to see my brother in the hospital, and he passed away. I did not understand that voice till later.

For Such a Time as This

As a young girl, I started believing that if God did not care for my brother by saving his life, that He would not care for me! My parents, rightfully so, were putting all their energy into taking care of the funeral and dealing with their own grief. Even though I was suffering and had gone through trauma, lacking my parents' attention led to me feeling invisible, and I started onto the bad road of people-pleasing and desperately wanting people's approval. It started with partying a little bit, leading to an eating disorder, then on to promiscuity, and to depression.

Every sin I tried never fulfilled my heart until I reached out to God. I said to God: "If you are really real please let me know and I will follow you wherever you want me to go." At that moment I had a huge peace come over me, and the Lord started speaking to me in my thoughts. When Jesus spoke, I knew that it was the same voice I heard the day my brother passed away. I also realized that when the Lord said my brother was going to be okay, that meant he was in heaven — a question my family and I wondered. Upon this profound realization at twenty, I made an art project about my brother and gave it to my parents. We all cried and celebrated, which was seven years later after my brother's death.

The moment God spoke to me, HE broke the Lie over me that I was insignificant, by making me realize He did care about me during my tragedy. He spoke to me about someone I truly loved (my brother) and showed me that He loved my brother more than I loved him.

God does not do that for everyone, but I do believe we all have moments when we know God is real, and He is who He says He is in the Bible. At the age of 20, I started seeking Him the best I knew how and started reading all those devotions my mom kept sending me at college. The Lord has taken me all over the world, and I have followed Him the best I can.

My path is definitely not perfect, but I know He is always with me, even in the fires of life. Isaiah 43:1 says, "You are Mine." So when I am down, I try to remind myself He always carries us when we are weak, sad, going through hard things, or even joyful times! Praise the Lord that I am HIS!

For Such a Time as This

GOD IS MY KEEPER

Throughout the Bible, God's people cry out to the Lord for help for various needs. Today we will look at one of God's names that we can call upon when we are in times of trouble – God our Keeper. Psalm 121 is focused on this facet of God's nature. God's people sang this Psalm each year when they journeyed to Jerusalem to worship the Lord in His temple. Jerusalem was surrounded by mountains so the trip to the holy city was strenuous and somewhat dangerous. Their hearts were strengthened with courage and hope as they sang the melodious declarations of God their Keeper.

The Psalm begins by telling the travelers to look up to the mountains, for they saw God's presence there (See Psalm 121:1). In focusing on the majestic mountains, they were reminded that God is the Maker of heaven and earth (See Psalm 121:2). On various occasions, I have traveled up high mountains. Looking upon the vastness of the terrain always gave me a sense of God's Almighty power. When you face challenges that seem overwhelming, look to the magnificent creation all around you to be reminded that He can take care of whatever you need.

Six times in this Psalm of only eight verses, we are told that God watches over us. "He will not let our foot slip – He who watches over you will not slumber" (See Psalm 121:4). This references that God would not allow the Israelites to fall in such a way that they could not get up again. Though many of us tend to be too independent at times and do things our own way; God is always attentive and will step in to prevent us from causing permanent damage to our souls.

"The Lord watches over you – the Lord is your shade at your right hand; the sun will not harm you by day, nor the moon by night" (See Psalm 121:5-6). This passage has a metaphorical meaning that God protects us as we journey through physical struggles (the sun) and emotional and psychological struggles (the moon). The Lord cares about every part of you. Whether you are battling cancer or some other physical ailment, wrestling with troubling emotions and thoughts, or striving to break away from an unhealthy behavior; God is with you to bring strength, healing, and freedom.

Whatever difficulty you are facing; the Lord is your Keeper. He is watching over your life to protect your soul and spirit from all harm. Your help comes from the Lord, the Maker of heaven and earth. Take a walk tonight and gaze at the vast expanse of the heavens as God reassures you that He is in control.

Today's Bible Reading: Psalm 121
By Sue Corl

For Such a Time as This

REMOVAL AND REPLANTING

"This is what the Sovereign LORD says: On the day I cleanse you from all your sins, I will resettle your towns, and the ruins will be rebuilt...Then the nations around you that remain will know that I the LORD have rebuilt what was destroyed and have replanted what was desolate. I the LORD have spoken, and I will do it" (Ezekiel 36:33, 36).

During the early morning in our booming Asian city last summer, we experienced rare typhoon-level winds and rain. Our area had seen flash floods like that before, but never with such powerful gusts of wind. Trees along the road and sidewalks were uprooted and turned completely on their side, dirt still clinging to their tendrils, blocking the usual thoroughfare of cars and passengers. Road crews immediately got to work clearing brush and debris.

Several days later as I walked through our neighborhood park, I observed what had been cleared and what was still being broken apart for removal and replanting. A potted tree whose pot had fallen on its side, its shards had been replaced and set aright; trees that once blocked the path were sawed into several large chunks, awaiting someone to carry them away for burning or recycling.

This past event now seems like a foreshadowing of what we are experiencing due to COVID-19. In a season of upheaval and extended waiting, what is Abba uprooting from our environments? What specifically is He removing and replanting in the hearts and lives of His people? How can we participate in this work of renewal? Whether Covid-19 or some other tragic event resulting in great suffering, we can know that God is present to restore and renew His people.

The people of Israel were uprooted from their own land due to blatantly dishonoring God's name among the nations. Their obvious denial of the greatness of God and continuous reliance upon idols resulted in their captivity by Assyria, then Babylon. It was the upheaval of the Babylonian empire 70 years later that ushered in a new era under Cyrus the Persian, under whose leadership the nation of Israel (then consisting of the tribes of Levi, Benjamin, and Judah) were allowed to return to their land and rebuild. Their rebellion and pride had been extreme, as was their punishment. Now God promised to restore them.

The God of Israel returned the rebellious nation of Judah to their home, and in the face of opposition helped them rebuild the city wall and Temple in Jerusalem. He restored the land to its former glory. If God did the work of total restoration for disobedient people, how much more does He desire to restore His obedient people, who are called to be His devoted servants among the nations of the world? If we, who desire to be witnesses of His fame among the nations, repent and return wholeheartedly to the sole Satisfier of our hearts, how much more will He pour out His presence on us in the most unlikely places of our cities and nations?

For Such a Time as This

What has God brought you out of in the past? Have you seen His deliverance before? If you sense chaos, upheaval, or uprooting in your environment, why not ask the Mighty Restorer of All Things to show you what He is planting? What new thing is He doing in you, through you? His restoration is long-lasting and complete. Take heart, beloved, the doors He opens, no man can shut.

> "This is what the Sovereign LORD says: On the day I cleanse you from all your sins, I will resettle your towns, and the ruins will be rebuilt...Then the nations around you that remain will know that I the LORD have rebuilt what was destroyed and have replanted what was desolate. I the LORD have spoken, and I will do it" (Ezekiel 36:33, 36).

Today's Bible Reading: Ezekiel 36: 16-28
By Julie Branstetter

GOD'S RESPONSE TO OUR FEARS

I love how God still loves us despite our sinful and fearful nature. In Genesis 27-35, we see the story of Jacob's life that is full of sin. Does God condemn and reject him? No. Jacob's name is often included in the Old Testament when God identifies Himself: "I am the God of Abraham, the God of Isaac, and the God of Jacob" (Exodus 3:15).

Jacob was a fearful man in many ways, whether his fear resulted from his own sinful ways, from his father-in-law, or his brother Esau. Jacob learned to seek the Lord during His time of duress. What I love is that God met with him, not in just little ways, but big ways too.

"I will protect you wherever you go" (Genesis 28:15).

"God told Laban (Jacob's father-in-law), 'I'm warning you, leave Jacob alone'" (Genesis 31:24). Jacob was not even aware that God was protecting him. When Laban went to see Jacob,

For Such a Time as This

he responded to Laban in fear.

"As Jacob started on his way again, angels of God came to meet him. When Jacob saw them, he said, 'This is God's camp'" (Genesis 32:1-2). Yet still he feared the revenge of his brother.

In fear, Jacob wrestled with the Angel of the Lord (God) and demanded a blessing (See Genesis 32:22-30).

Jacob's life can encourage us as we experience our own challenges. We go through life and things happen that cause us to get worried and scared. Perhaps you are in a difficult season right now. We forget that God has already brought us through many difficult days. He's helped us in sickness, financial problems, and poor decisions we made in our past. Yet, at every turn, we still are uncertain.

I want to encourage you if you are fearful to rest in the Lord's blessings of peace. No matter how many times we get fearful or worried, He is there for us holding our hand through every situation. Don't let the enemy cast shame on you for your humanity. God is patient with our troubled emotions and welcomes our honest prayers. Rather than focusing on media, fix your eyes on the One who will walk with you through this season. God loves you so much and desires to lead you step by step.

May the God of Abraham, the God of Isaac and the God of Jacob bless you beyond your heart's desire today with His love and peace.

Today's Bible Reading: Genesis 27-35.
By Tyla Kozub

A BEAUTIFUL SPRING TREE OF HOPE

I was having a prayer walk when God impressed upon me to look at a fully blooming pink and white tree. Immediately, I saw half of the blooming flowers on the ground still beautiful and full of color, and the other half of blooms still on the tree. It was a beautiful sight! The Holy Spirit brought the words of Jesus to my mind. "Very truly I tell you, unless a kernel of wheat falls to the ground and dies, it remains only a single seed. But if it dies, it produces many seeds" (John 12:24, NLT).

God was reminding me just how beautiful life is, and when we know Him as Lord and Savior, the promise of heaven after death is even more wonderful. God has called us to be in this world for such a time as this. We can trust that He will take care of our every need. So many of us are mourning for loved ones, close friends, or even distant unknowns. Grieving is hard. And we will go through the grief cycle sometimes many times a day as we hear about sorrowful and despairing

For Such a Time as This

situations. But may we remember this: God has a welcoming party and feast for those coming to their true home in heaven. It will be glorious!

Those of us left behind, God has us on a pause button to stay and do a NEW thing for Him. I encourage you to seek Him for any changes He might want you to make. We should not long for the old but look forward to the new. "For unless a kernel of wheat falls to the ground and dies, it remains only a single seed. But if it dies, it produces many seeds" (John 12:24).

What has the world's chaos changed in your life? What areas need to die, so God can produce fruit from you? As we seek this new season together, let us pray how we can be effective for the Lord in ways we never thought possible. For God is the God of the impossible!!! He loves to do things beyond our thinking. He is the miracle worker. When this season passes, let us not just go back to our old ways. Let us continue to move in the new things God has challenged us to do during this season.

Lord, thank you for today!! I ask you to comfort my sisters and brothers in Christ who are suffering losses. Please help them to finish everything they need to get done and guide them step-by-step. And for us who are waiting on this season to be over, let us consider the new and honor the old. What do you have for the church? How can we think differently? We love you, Lord. Help us live in the New!

Today's Bible reading: John 12:20-36
By Tyla Kozub

SHAKAN!
AN UNUSAL BATTLE WORD

Shakan! Doesn't that sound like some word that explodes from the screen when a Power Ranger knocks down the enemy! I admit, I used to watch Power Rangers with my son when he was a little boy. He would put on his Power Ranger suit and then jump out in front of his little sister, thrusting his arms and fists mightily before her and say, "Stop, you will never get past me!"

Moses used this powerful Hebrew word shakan when he prayed for the tribe of Benjamin in Deuteronomy 33:12.

> "Let the beloved of the Lord rest (shakan) secure in Him, for He shields him all day long, and the one the Lord loves rests (shakan) between His shoulders."

Notice that in one sentence he used shakan twice: "shakan secure in Him" and "shakan" between His shoulders. In Hebrew, the word shakan means rest, to dwell, to settle down, to abide, to set in place. Think of the last time you used super glue to set something permanently in place. Within seconds, it fastens two objects together preventing them from ever separating again (an unfortunate quality when we accidentally super glue our two fingers together!).

Moses prays for Benjamin's tribe to rest (shakan) securely in God. The word secure in Hebrew is betach. It is defined as "safety, security, a place of refuge, related both to the fact of security and the feeling of trust, a place of assurance, without care, confidence, and hope" (The Hebrew Interlinear Bible online, Blue Letter Bible.org). What an encouraging phrase for us all as the world is experiencing so many calamities. We can confidently trust in Him, knowing that He is in control and has supernatural power!

Moses knows that the Israelites will go through many battles with the enemy throughout their lives. So he exhorts them to rest in God. Jesus tells us the same thing in John 15:4-11. We are to be super glued to Him! We are to be grafted into the vine. He says to be glued to His Word and to His love, "For apart from Him, we can do nothing" (John 15:5). As we do this, we will experience His love and joy.

Let's go back to Deuteronomy 33:12 and fix our eyes on the beautiful word pictures Moses gives us. As we rest in the Lord, He will shield us 24/7. Nothing gets through the impenetrable shield of God (see Ephesians 6:16). In Deuteronomy 33:14, Moses gives us a picture of resting between God's shoulders. Observe what the Lord says about the ones who are resting. He says they are "the beloved of the Lord, the one the Lord loves." That is us! God's children. "How great is the love the Father has lavished on us, that we should be called children of God!" (1 John 3:1).

My husband and I raised our two children near the beach. When they were young, we would take them to swim in the ocean. They loved it when we would put them on our shoulders and walk out into deeper waters. When the waves would come crashing down, they would squeal in delight (only getting their legs wet) while Mom and Dad got pounded by the waves! God wants to lift you up on His shoulders. Abide and rest in Him. Let Him absorb the pounding waves of the enemy. Then squeal in delight over His love and protection.

Sisters and brothers, God loves you very much. He wants you to rest in Him. Stay "super-glued" to God! When you feel the enemy attack you with fear, raise up your arms and shout "Shakan!" Yes, rest in the Lord. Let Him be the One to flood you with peace. Let Him be the One to place you upon His shoulders. Let Him be the One to fight the battles. And don't forget to pray this beautiful prayer of Moses for others: "Let the beloved of the Lord rest secure in Him, for He shields him all day long, and the one the Lord loves rests between His shoulders" (Deuteronomy 33:12).

Today's Bible Reading: Deuteronomy 33:12, 14 and
John 15:4-11
By Sue Corl

For Such a Time as This

HE CALLS US TO BE CHILDREN

My three kids asked a lot of questions when they were little. "Mommy, why did God make the sun yellow? Is peanut butter a vegetable? Why do I have to make my bed? I will be using it again in a few hours!" It drove me crazy sometimes, but I tried hard to answer them the best I could.

During uncertain times, we ask a lot of questions. Some of us feel we should not bother God with our doubts or "trivial" questions. But He is our Father, our Daddy! He wants us to come to Him. In fact, He appreciates a childlike faith.

"Jesus called a little child and had him stand among them. And He said: 'I tell you the truth, unless you change and become like little children, you will never enter the kingdom of heaven. Therefore, whoever humbles himself like this child is the greatest in the kingdom of heaven" (Matthew 18:2-3).

He is not annoyed by our barrage of questions, even ones we think are silly or question His Word. As we come to God with those hard questions, He will answer in ways that grow our faith. He may not always answer them the way we want

Him to, but He loves to give us wisdom. The Father also loves to listen to us! Be patient and persistent. His answers may not come in your timing. There are some mysteries that are beyond our comprehension. I praise God that one day we will stand before the Lord in heaven and finally understand the answers to our "why" questions.

When we see everything that is going on around us, it is easy to question if God is who He says He is. Again, He is not annoyed by your questions. Remember when we first began to follow Jesus? We were just "babes in Christ." 1 Corinthians 3:2 uses this analogy to describe how God first teaches us the basics of our faith. "I gave you milk, not solid food, for you were not yet ready for it." Over time, we gain more understanding of who God is and His will for us. We grow stronger in our faith.

However, during tough times, we can fall back into questioning God. It is okay to be honest with our struggles and questions, but do not give into lies about God. "Go back to what you heard and believed at first; hold to it firmly. Repent and turn to me again" (Revelation 3:3). God is who He says He is in the Word. His promises are true. His ways are trustworthy. He is the same yesterday, today, and tomorrow.

I can remember times when my daughter would not stop asking me a million questions. After answering several of them, I finally picked her up in my arms, held her tight, and said, "I love you my wonderful, smart, adorable daughter." Suddenly, all of her questions stopped. She smiled as she soaked in my love. She felt safe. The world was still full of mysteries, but she knew the most important thing: she was loved and cared for.

Let God sweep you up in His arms and comfort you. Rest in Him. "As my Father has loved me, so have I loved you. Now remain in my love" (John 15:9).

For Such a Time as This

We love you Jesus so much! Thank you for helping us with every step today. May we feel your love as a hen protects her chicks! Amen and Amen.

Today's Bible Reading: Romans 8:14-17; Mark 10:13-16.
By Tyla Kozub and Sue Corl

Crown of Beauty International

GRIEVING BRINGS HOPE

Part IV

For Such a Time as This

NOT WHY, BUT HOW?

The story of Joseph's suffering and God's redeeming hand takes place in Genesis 37-50. He experienced great pain as his own brothers sold him into slavery, which led to the loss of his family, homeland, livelihood, and enslavement. Even when he gained respect as a slave, he found himself thrown into jail unjustly. Joseph was probably asking God: Why?

As we read his story, we see that Joseph did not get an answer for many years, but God did bless him as he became a powerful leader in Egypt due to the gifting of his dreams. When a famine struck the lands, Joseph helped Egypt be ready and his position led to reconciliation between himself and his brothers, paving a way for him to save not only the Egyptians but his family too. I have always been awestruck by his statement to his brothers after the death of their father, Jacob: "You intended to harm me, but God intended it for good to accomplish what is now being done, the saving of many lives" (Genesis 50:20). It points to a truth that is both beautiful and difficult; as we walk through a challenging season, we probably will not know why it happened (and that is painful), but we can rest in the assurance that God will redeem our suffering.

When I have faced crises, I find myself asking: Why? Why did I have to leave my home? Why is my mother's health suffering? Why are my friends hurting? Why; it is the most frequent question we ask as we struggle and wrestle through the uncertainties, our emotions, and the tidal waves of life. But why often doesn't get answered in the moments we want it to. When I ask this question, I find I have dug myself into a dark hole. I spiral deeper and deeper, getting temporary relief as my mind is occupied by imagining an answer to why, but then realize I have wandered so far from the light. There is a time and place for digging this hole, because honestly, only when I am in it, do I truly feel and understand the weight of the circumstances I am experiencing. But I shouldn't stay there forever — for if I do, I give room for despair, depression, and utter desolation to set root in my soul.

After we have grieved and asked why, we must ask how. How will God redeem this? How will God restore us? There is hope in this question. As I reflect on how, I climb out of the hole, not only thinking of how God will redeem this situation that got me in this hole, but I think of how He redeemed and restored ALL the difficult circumstances I faced before.

I challenge you, as you walk away from this devotional, to continue to reflect and grieve, but most importantly push into asking God how. I believe that God will reveal the answer to how, as you dive deep and ask Him. You might not know why, but I really truly believe God always shows us how. I want to leave you with this hope.

Today's Bible Reading: Genesis 37-50.
By Kaelah Byrom

For Such a Time as This

GOD NEVER LET'S US GO
Kaelah Byrom's Testimony

I had a very unusual upbringing. My American parents raised me overseas in Bosnia and Herzegovina. Before the age of twenty-one, I had moved seventeen times and been to nine different schools. Even now, I find myself haunted by people I wish I still knew. Though there are many stories I could share, the one that has had the biggest effect on my life is my eating disorder.

Before I turned twenty, I had thirteen different therapists who all asked me the same question: What caused your anorexia? I could come up with several reasons. Perhaps it was the culture shock of America and how its school systems put a heavy emphasis on ending childhood obesity. Before 5th grade, I had barely thought about my weight in such away. Maybe it was my grandmother's aid as she weighed and measured me, helping me lose whatever little baby fat I did have in fifth grade. Or it could have been how out of control my world felt as I moved back and forth between cities of Bosnia and the United States. I had gained and lost friends and homes many times. More likely it is a combination of all these things. I remember when the habits began, cutting carbs and skipping meals, I told myself it was just for a month. If only I had known then that I was setting myself up for an eight-year battle.

An eating disorder is a form of addiction. When there is an addict in a family, it is not only the addict who suffers but the entire family. It wreaks havoc, ripping and tearing everything good apart. I hate to say it about myself, but I became unrecognizable, practically a monster. Between 6th grade and 10th grade, I was severely bullied and kicked out of school. I had lost my home (Bosnia), gone to rehab, and moved to Wisconsin. Shame latched on to my heart in those years, it even to this day can creep up on me in my weakest moments. When my parents sat my sisters and me down to tell us we would not be going back to Bosnia because I was still too sick, my sisters looked me in the eye and told me they would never forgive me.

In those years, I tried so hard. I remember begging God to heal me, but He never did. I hated having people pray for me to be healed and experiencing the disappointment when I wasn't once again. I grew frustrated with myself for not having enough faith and with God for not having enough grace to heal me.

There was a night when I was so done with the conflicts in my family and with the voice of the eating disorder in my head. I lay contemplating taking my own life, with a knife in my hand listening to a Christian Pandora station on shuffle. I had been to this deep place of despair before but never had I so seriously desired to take my own life. I felt that God had abandoned me. I was a burden and disappointment to my family. I sobbed on the floor listening. Just when I was ready to act, Never Let Go by David Crowder Band played. It was a song that we often played in the chapel at Rehab, but I never knew the name of it. I had searched the internet for it many times with no luck at finding it. The song meant a lot to me as it had brought me comfort in my times at the rehab center. I truly believe it was God speaking to me as I planned to take my life. I broke into awful sobs, feeling as if God's hand had reached out to hold me.

I have always experienced God actively moving throughout my life. In the mornings when I woke up, I would sit talking with Jesus. But I had never known the trouble as deep as my heart knew then. This moment was a clean and clear reminder that God had not left — would never leave me, and had a good plan for me even though my life sucked at that moment.

I was never miraculously healed, to my great disappointment. It took me a long time to realize that maybe an instant healing was just not in God's plans for me and that had nothing to do with my faith or walk with God. In fact, nearly thirteen years since I became sick with anorexia, I have seen God pull me closer to Him and draw those struggling with food and their own mental health towards me. Those who were instantly healed were never able to empathize with me, but after eight years of fighting to be free of the eating disorder, I now know what it is to struggle.

The greatest advice I have ever been given is a metaphor of a car stuck in the snow. When you're driving forward and get stuck, sometimes you have to drive backwards to be able to get out. On the path to healing, there will be mistakes and slip-ups, but that doesn't mean you can't keep moving forward when they happen. I encourage and bless you all on your individual journeys to healing. Listen to the song if you've never heard of it. I pray you walk away from my story knowing that God never lets us go.

HOPE BEYOND THE LAMENT

With each passing day that we find ourselves in the midst of a world plagued with suffering, the brokenness both within and around us has become certain and plain. The reality is that none of us right now are devoid of the aching language of an afflicted soul, crying out for relief and hope. The greater reality is that we have a Savior who has endured suffering and affliction to the point of death, even death upon a cross. He is a Savior identified as a man of sorrow, acquainted with grief (See Isaiah 53:3). A Savior familiar with the language of lament, inviting us to become familiar with this language as well.

Listen to the anguished heart of the psalmist in Psalm 22:1-4 — a psalm of lament predicting the sufferings of Jesus.

> "My God, my God, why have you forsaken me? Why are you so far from saving me, from the words of my

groaning? O my God, I cry by day, but you do not answer, and by night, but I find no rest. Yet you are holy, enthroned on the praises of Israel. In you our fathers trusted; they trusted, and you delivered them. To you they cried and were rescued; in you they trusted and were not put to shame."

The psalm is quoted by our Lord Jesus as He hung upon the cross, as if it were His own, candid, raw, unfiltered feelings before God. Notice grief and affliction were not a position of silence but rather of coming to God, speaking out boldly with deep and honest expressions of the soul.

I am increasingly convinced that God is inviting His people, for such a time as this, to personally learn and engage in the language of lament. Webster's Dictionary defines lament as, "to mourn aloud: wail." For the Christian, our lamentation is directed toward a person, God, whose desire is to intimately engage with us in the afflictions and suffering of day to day life. Our lament is not purely mourning before the Lord or crying out in hopeless pain and despair; it is an act of trust placed in God, knowing that He hears and cares about the cries of His people. Lament ushers us into a deeper position of trust before the Lord, recounting who He is — who He has always been to His people.

When we commemorate Jesus' death on the cross, we become uncomfortably aware of the stench of death within our cities and communities. May the hope of what lies ahead of us strengthen our own lamentations by "looking to Jesus, the founder and perfecter of our faith, who for the joy that was set before Him endured the cross, despising the shame, and is seated at the right hand of the throne of God" (Hebrews 12:2). Jesus tasted joy in the midst of His suffering. Jesus had hope engulfed in His lament. The joy of a restored relationship with us was worth His death upon a sinner's cross, even if He had to bear being separated from the Father. He endured God's wrath poured onto Him for our sin. But the joy of a restored relationship with us gave Him the strength to endure the trial.

We know that joy is a fruit of the Spirit (See Galatians 5:22-23). If you have joy today, even in the midst of sorrow surrounding you, don't feel guilty. There is joy available for us, for we know that God has a purpose in which He will use evil to bring about good. He is already bringing many throughout the world to Himself. He is softening hearts and opening eyes and ears to consider what life is really about, what comes after death, and what hope there is for us. We know that Jesus is the answer to these questions. May we journey during this time of affliction near to our Risen Savior, even in the midst of lamentation. For we know that hope is found in Him.

Today's Bible Reading: Isaiah 53; Psalm 22; Lamentations 3
By Nancy Martin

For Such a Time as This

IT'S OKAY TO NOT BE OKAY

When we look to the individuals of the Bible, like Job, David, Naomi, and Hannah, we see how several experienced pain and allowed themselves to go to the deep hurts of their hearts. This is very different than what society sometimes tells us to do when we face trials and struggles. I would argue that God wants us to grieve well. Job, David, Naomi, and Hannah all mourned their pains in the Bible, and none of them received punishment for allowing themselves to feel their pain; in fact, they were blessed by God in one way or another. God does not expect us to hide how we feel from Himself or others.

Job experiences some of the greatest suffering imaginable as he lost his family, wealth, health, land, and eventually the support of his own friends. Though Job never dishonors God, he speaks freely of his suffering and eventually claims that he wishes he was never born and curses that day in a long poetic speech (See Job 3). As for David, the Psalms account for his mourning over and over again. He grieves the death of his infant son and the consequences of his actions with Bathsheba (See 2 Samuel 12:13-25). When Abner died, David commands all those with him to mourn by tearing their clothes and wearing sack cloths (See 2 Samuel 3:30-35). His songs are full of his lament.

Naomi, having lost her sons and husband, renames herself, Mara, meaning bitter. She takes on an attitude of grief as she returns to her homeland.

Hannah gives another example of grieving well in the Bible. At the temple, she cries so deeply out to the Lord for a child that Eli mistakes her for a drunk, but her grieving is blessed, and God gives her a son (See 1 Samuel 1:5-20).

Even when we look to Christ, the One we are setting our hearts to be most like, we see that He grieved and let Himself go to the places where His heart ached. When Lazarus died, "Jesus wept" (John 11:35). At the Garden of Gethsemane, Jesus tells his disciples that his "soul is overwhelmed with sorrow to the point of death" (Matthew 26:38). Even Jesus did not shy away from His pain.

When I look at these stories of how Biblical characters and our Lord Jesus Christ dealt with suffering, I am moved to experience my grief more fully. This world is filled with suffering. But for so long, we have glazed over our own and others' pains, becoming increasingly desensitized to poverty, violence, and the needs of this world. How could we not, when the needs cry out so great that to see them fully would honestly break our hearts? Only with Jesus can we grieve for ourselves and the world fully, for the burden will not fall on us - it will be carried by Jesus. Jesus wants to dig down deep in our mess and weep with us. We just need to give Him the space to start working.

Today's Bible Reading: Job 3, 2 Samuel 12; Luke 22.
By Kaelah Byrom

THE BEAUTY OF WAITING

I have been considering our ability — and inability — to wait at critical times.

I remember growing anxious during my assigned internship in college. I was becoming impatient because I had nothing to do for several days (and I like to do!). After talking to my professor about it, she advised that I wait and let her handle the situation. I did not wait. I took the matter into my own hands and spoke to my supervisor about it directly. My professor was NOT happy!

As insecure human beings, we have a tendency to want to feel in control, to know what is happening at certain stages, to see the unseen progress, even to create progress if none is apparent. I have been an expert at this at times. But prayer and a faithful Father have changed that. I have seen Him work miracles as a result of waiting. Wisdom has taught me that HIS timing is not only perfect, it's essential for His perfect work!

I recall how at the beginning of this year my husband and I

thought we had our plans all worked out. We thought we knew 'The Plan,' but world events have changed everything: our family's location, our kids' schooling, who we are quarantined with, and our next steps. I continue to wait for His revelation, His timing, and His direction.

When I meditate on the resurrection of Jesus, I am reminded that Abba's timing is absolutely perfect. How thankful I am that while Jesus was hanging on the cross, He trusted Abba's redemptive plan and timing! He had to be in the grave over the Sabbath to force people to REST after the work of redemption had been completed. The women who followed His body to the tomb on Friday night returned on Sunday morning with spices in hand. Instead, they found an empty tomb!

Let's stop right there for a moment. PAUSE. Rest.

Ah, the joy of knowing the end of the story! I smile with content delight, knowing that they are about to discover the most earth-shattering, life-changing event in all of history! An event that previously, they had no idea would happen. Luke 24:4a says, "They stood there puzzled."

How many times have we stood at life's crossroads and felt puzzled because we did not know the unseen facts? We did not know that Abba had already worked the plan out for us in advance. We stand there dumbfounded because it looks like a door slammed in our faces. We have forgotten that He has already gone before us and prepared a way, a better way, a miraculous way. We have forgotten that He is good — ALL THE TIME. Sometimes we assume that not knowing is the same as having no reason to trust. Our Abba always goes ahead and works out the plan in advance. "I will send my angel ahead of you to prepare the way for you" (Exodus 32:34).

How many times have we recognized, after the fact, that we almost missed Him and His providential timing? Why?

For Such a Time as This

Because our minds were too dull and we doubted. The Resurrection reminds us that HE has a purpose in everything that happens, and it is GOOD, because HE is good! He has made everything beautiful in its time" (Ecclesiastes. 3:11).

Lord God, I thank You that You are entirely faithful! You know the pathway we are to take, and You are working out the details and provision for the journey, even now. Father, thank you for shaking up my plans so I can receive Your plan! Awaken my heart to be ready to recognize what You are doing and to cooperate with the Holy Spirit's guidance. In Jesus' Name I pray, Amen.

> "Be still in the presence of the LORD and wait patiently for him to act" (Psalm 37:7a).

Today's Bible Reading: Luke 24:1-12
By Julie Bransetter

THE SECRET OF CONTENTMENT

"I know what it is to be in need, and I know what it is to have plenty. I have learned the secret of being content in any and every situation, whether well fed or hungry, whether living in plenty or in want" (Philippians 4:12).

Paul says that he has learned the secret of being content. His contentment was not dependent on his circumstances. He had been in some incredibly tough times, yet still had joy. In fact, when he wrote this passage, he was in prison. In 2 Corinthians 11:23-28, he experiences more difficulties and stress than most people ever endure, and yet, Paul was able to say he was content.

I want to suggest that there are three facets to the secret of contentment. In Philippians 4:13, Paul says, "I can do everything through Him who gives me strength." Every day, Paul totally relied on the Lord for the strength to face whatever came his way. He knew that "apart from God he could do nothing" (John 15:5). In fact, Paul grew to realize that it was because of his weaknesses and hardships that he was growing in faith and Christ-like character (See 2 Corinthians 12:10). Trials humble us and can bring us to a place of deeper dependency on God. This in turn helps us grow in maturity. I encourage you to read Philippians 3. It is here that we see Paul's passion to know Christ and His power. The more he experienced the love and power of the Spirit of Christ, the more he endured hardships with great joy.

The second part of the secret is woven throughout Philippians; he continually gave thanks and rejoiced in whatever God brought into His life (Philippians 4:4-7). He said that the act of rejoicing is a safeguard to us (Philippians 3:1). When we give thanks in the midst of pain and suffering, it protects us from spiraling into a state of despair and hopelessness. Giving thanks in these situations is not ignoring or suppressing our troubled emotions. It is okay, and even healthy to honestly admit our sadness and grief. Giving thanks is an acknowledgment by faith that God is good, present, and in control. Paul gave thanks while in prison because He knew that ultimately, God's will and plan is good. It may not seem that way to us, but God is sovereign over all things. He has an eternal plan that not even Satan can thwart. His plans will ultimately bring His Kingdom. "He will wipe away every tear from their eyes. There will be no more death or mourning or crying or pain, for the old order of things has passed away (Revelation 21:4).

When we bring our burdens to God, He will carry them, and give us comfort and peace (See Matthew 11:28-30). I have personally experienced, heard and read endless testimonies of the power of praise changing us and our circumstances. One of my favorite testimonies is from a village in Pakistan. A church was destroyed by terrorists. The pastor immediately called his congregation together to worship, forgive the men who bombed their building, and give thanks to God. Some refused and were too bitter to participate in this time of prayer. However, most participated and as they did, their hearts were filled with hope and joy. Within that week, many Muslim villagers came to the pastor to learn of this Jesus that gave them a forgiving and thankful heart. They too wanted to experience this kind of God! When we engage in thanksgiving, there seems to be a supernatural anointing from God that comes over us and the situation we are experiencing, that not only lifts our spirit, but also brings about significant positive change.

Paul's third secret of contentment relates to surrendering everything to God. Paul considered all personal riches, accomplishments, titles, and profits as rubbish compared to knowing Christ (See Philippians 3:7-11). He lived his life completely for the glory of God and not for his own personal gain. He knew that His true joy and satisfaction came from knowing the riches of the love of Christ. This is why he prayed for the believers in Ephesus to know the depth of God's love so that they could be "filled to the measure of all the fullness of God" (Ephesians 3:17-19).

You will discover that utter surrender to God will bring you the greatest joy. The Lord knows what is best for us. He created us! He knows our DNA! He knows everything about us — in fact, He knows us better than we know ourselves. We can trust Him with every detail of our lives. Jesus says that He came to give us an abundant and extraordinary life (See John 10:10). Surrender and trust may not always be easy, but ultimately, they will bring us to a place of contentment.

Today's Bible Reading: Philippians 3, 4:11-13;
2 Corinthians 12:7-10.
By Sue Corl

For Such a Time as This

WHAT IS THE MEANING OF LIFE?

King Solomon, though blessed by God with great wisdom, became obsessed with the question, "What is the meaning of life?" He pursued one thing after another: wealth, women, and grand projects like building extraordinary gardens and houses. He studied the universe; and sought to grow in the knowledge of complex physical and sociological matters. He poured himself into experiencing the pleasures of wine, music, food, and purchasing extravagant treasures. With each pursuit, his heart was empty, and he felt his life was meaningless.

One thought deeply troubled Solomon's spirit — no matter how people live, in the end, they die. King Solomon was despairing due to his uncertainty of what happens to people after they die (See Ecclesiastes 3:20-21). Though he hoped his spirit would live on and be in the presence of God, he did not have this assurance, thus at times feelings of hopelessness overwhelmed him.

Perhaps you too are struggling with feelings of meaninglessness. When the troubles of this world overwhelm us, or we experience mental or physical illness, we can begin to question many things about our lives. This led King Solomon to even question his eternal life. If this is part of your struggle, take courage sisters and brothers, the Lord promises us eternal life through the sacrificial blood of Christ.

> "For God so loved the world that He gave His one and only Son, that whoever believes in Him shall not perish but have eternal life" (John 3:16).

We are eternal beings, given life on this earth as only the beginning of a beautiful eternal journey with our Lord.

As I thought about Solomon's despair over the deeper questions of life and death, I realized that we have freedom from this fear. In fact, Solomon's conclusion to his quest is the very thing that can motivate us and gives us purpose! Jesus enlightens us to see that our purpose and fulfillment are not found in earthly treasures, but in eternal gain.

> "Do not store up for yourselves treasures on earth, where moth and rust destroy, and where thieves break in and steal. But store up for yourselves treasures in heaven, where moth and rust do not destroy, and where thieves do not break in and steal. For where your treasure is, there your heart will be also" (Matthew 6:19-21).

When we go through suffering, we can feel life is meaningless. Why do I need to be in such pain? When will this stop? I am tired of this trial! I want it to end! I feel useless. What is the point of it all? Do you struggle with some of these thoughts?

There is no easy answer to the questions about suffering.

For Such a Time as This

As we bring these questions before the Lord, He will often give us some answers that bring peace of mind. Let's go on in our reading of Ecclesiastes to see what brought peace to Solomon.

Solomon had a sense of the significance of eternity. He said:

> "He has set eternity in the hearts of men; yet they cannot fathom what God has done from beginning to end" (Ecclesiastes 3:11).

As Christ had not yet come, Solomon had a limited understanding of his eternal purpose on earth. However, he ends his dissertation of "the meaning of life" with these words:

> "Now all has been heard; here is the conclusion of the matter; Fear God and keep His commandments, for this is the whole duty of man. For God will bring every deed into judgment, including every hidden thing, whether it is good or evil" (Ecclesiastes 12:13-14).

This is great advice. We are eternal beings! God has placed us on this earth to grow in our relationship with Him, become more like Christ, worship and glorify Him, and make Him known to others. This is a time of preparation for the wonderful eternal life we will have in God's presence. No matter how difficult, painful, or mundane our life may seem at times, it is not meaningless. When we live according to His will for the eternal purpose of glorifying God, all things have meaning!

I can rejoice when I know I am doing the things that God wants me to do. I give thanks and take joy because I know my Lord is pleased with me. We have the Holy Spirit dwelling within us giving us spiritual connection with God, understanding of His Word, and power to live a life pleasing to God. Bringing delight to the heart of God and experiencing loving fellowship with Him is the most significant part of our existence.

Today's Bible Reading: Ecclesiastes 3, Ecclesiastes 12
By Sue Corl

For Such a Time as This

AUTHORS

Sue Corl is an International Women's Conference speaker, author, mentor, and Bible teacher. She is the founder and director of Crown of Beauty International and Beauty for Ashes Conferences (https://crownofbeautyintl.wixsite.com/crownofbeauty). Sue is the author of *Crown of Beauty Bible Study, Crown of Beauty Leader's Guide, More Beautiful by the Day, and Mission Impossible*. Her greatest joy is being a wife and mother to two adult children. She has a passion for seeing women transformed by God's deep love. She served as a missionary for 25 years in Asia. Currently, she travels to minister to women throughout Asia, Africa, the Middle East, and the U.S. She has a Master's of Education from the University of Hawaii and a Master's of Christian Counseling from Philadelphia Biblical University.

Nancy Martin joined the Crown of Beauty International team in 2017 serving as the Social Media Director, conference speaker, and mentor of millennial and Gen Z women. Her passion is to pursue Jesus and help women to find life and freedom through truth. Currently, she travels to minister to women throughout Asia, Africa, the Middle East, and the U.S. She has a B.S. in Bible with a focus in Missions from Carin University and is certified in Biblical Counseling from Westminster Theological Seminary.

Julie Branstetter is a lover of Jesus who is passionate about growing others in knowing God intimately through His Word, prayer, and redemptive relationships. She is married to her best friend Chris, and through their living in Asia, has been actively engaged in growing a supportive, transformative community of families of kids with special needs. Together, she and Chris have two daughters.

Tyla Kozub lives in the Philadelphia area with her husband and three children. She graduated from Virginia Commonwealth University and has her certificate degree from Westminster Theological Seminary in Biblical Counseling. She and her husband have church planted in Hawaii and Asia for the last twenty years. Currently, Tyla is a teacher and mentor with Crown of Beauty International ministries. She has a deep passion for women ministry leaders to become free in Christ.

Kaelah Byrom is an aspiring writer who began creating stories at the age of six. At the age of sixteen, she self-published a fantasy novel, The Lost City, and has since furthered her writing career by earning a degree in English and continuously seeking to publish her novels. She also has a unique understanding and appreciation for the world, as she spent her childhood overseas in Bosnia and Herzegovina. Kaelah's exposure to different perspectives and difficult circumstances has given her an empathetic and hopeful heart for the ways God brings about His goodness out of the brokenness in this world.

For Such a Time as This

ENDORSEMENTS

"These are crazy times. Staying calm and steady each day is a challenge. For Such a Time as This is an offering to help you walk through the crisis of loss, isolation, challenge, and uncertainty with the God who's ever near. Sue Corl's gathered other voices to compile an easy-to-read devotional that feels like a familiar voice and a strengthening, intimate hug, with the reminder: Together we'll make it through."
—**Nancy Hicks**, Author of Meant to Live

"A Spirit-filled, biblically-focused, and uplifting devotional that inspires transformational thinking centered on God's presence and sovereign power during these troubling times."
— **Deneen McDonald** - a Church Leader and Advocate for Women

"For Such a Time As This, Walking through Crisis is a timely devotional written by women who are transparent about their own difficult experiences. Each devotional draws insight from Scripture and encourages the reader to cling to God in the face of all kinds of crises."
— **Cas Monaco**, Cru City Executive Director, author of Astonishing Love

Crown of Beauty International

OTHER BOOKS
By Sue Corl, Crown of Beauty International

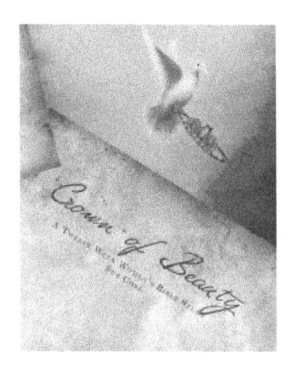

Crown of Beauty
A Twelve Week Women's
Bible Study

Crown of Beauty
Leader's Guide

More Beautiful
By The Day
A Devotional

Mission Impossible:
A Journey of Faith
with the Characters of
Hebrew 11